JENNIFER CLARKE was born in 1933 in Cairo, Egypt where both her parents taught. She studied at the Royal Academy of Dramatic Art in London and worked as an actress for several years. Later she lived in Scotland and then in Wales where she taught drama at Dyfed College of Art in Carmarthen. Returning to London, she became a registered London Tourist Board guide. She now works in the publicity department of the Barbican Arts Centre. She loves to walk, swim, read and travel, and has one daughter who is an artist.

JOANNA PARKIN was born in Swansea in 1938, and from 1955–57 studied photography at the Regent Street Polytechnic. She then spent two years as a staff photographer for the *Slough Observer*. Since 1961 she has worked as a freelance photographer for various national newspapers and magazines. She now lives in Hampton Hill, Middlesex with her husband and three children, and describes her greatest treat as their holidays in Scotland, as far away as possible from people and traffic.

Jennifer Clarke and Joanna Parkin are sisters, and they have included their mother, Gwen Clarke, an Infant School teacher and later headmistress, in *In Our Grandmothers' Footsteps*.

NOTE

All those who want to walk in *Grandmothers' Footsteps* will find at the back of the book a breakdown of London into areas, and under each will be listed the women whose memorials, plaques, gravestones, etc., are to be found in that area.

IN OUR GRANDMOTHERS' FOOTSTEPS

—

JENNIFER CLARKE

—

PHOTOGRAPHS BY
JOANNA PARKIN

In memory of our mother, Gwen Clarke
and dedicated to
Robin, Emma, David and Kate,
Julia and Nick and Waldo Clarke.

Published by VIRAGO PRESS Limited 1984
41 William IV Street, London WC2N 4DB

Text copyright © Jennifer Clarke 1984

Illustrations copyright © Joanna Parkin 1984

British Library Cataloguing in Publication Data
Clarke, Jennifer
    In our grandmothers' footsteps.
    1. Memorials – England – London – Guide books – 1951
    2. Women
    I. Title   II. Parkin, Joanna
    942.1'009'92   DA689.M7
    ISBN 0-86068-371-0

Photoset by Rowland Phototypesetting Ltd,
Bury St Edmunds, Suffolk
and printed in Great Britain

PREFACE

When we began this book, we were simply interested in the fact that among the hundreds of statues in the streets, squares and parks of London, we could find only eight monuments to women. We had not, at this point, included statues of queens (who had, we felt, an unfair advantage anyway), nor had we looked *inside* buildings. So – where were all the others?

A closer scrutiny provided endless clues – memorials tucked away in churches, plaques on houses, graves in sprawling cemeteries, statues in quiet corners of museums, and portraits in art galleries. A long, straggling procession of women began to emerge. Some were still famous, others had been neglected, many came as a complete surprise.

All the women here have some connection, however tenuous, with London, and all of them are dead. A few brazen characters pushed their way in and tried to take over, several queens, no doubt using the royal prerogative, insisted on being included and actresses and writers tended to dominate. We have made a deliberate attempt to trace 'others' and there are women who have murdered, or consorted with murderers, women who have 'used' men, or been used by them, women who were brilliant, restless, arrogant, stupid or selfish – and women who masqueraded successfully as men.

As we finished we were left with mixed feelings – of great regret that so many had to be left on the shelf (we have only scratched the surface), of respect for their courage, persistence, sense of humour and talent, and, above all, perhaps, of the delight and enjoyment that we gained by coming into close contact with their 'infinite variety'.

ACKNOWLEDGEMENTS

We would like to acknowledge, with love and gratitude, the great help and encouragement given to us throughout the making of this book by D. Waldo Clarke, lecturer, author, and also our father.

Our thanks are also due to all those friends, relations, colleagues and acquaintances who lent us their books, gave us invaluable clues, delved into their memories and gave practical help in every possible way.

For other particular help and advice, we wish to thank David Doughan of the Fawcett Library; George Glenton; Lieutenant-Colonel Cyril Barnes of the Salvation Army Headquarters in London; Ellis Plaice; Mrs Williamson, Deputy-Head of Owen's School, Potters Bar; Mrs Eric Fraser; The Royal Humane Society; Bill Robson; Mr Robinson, Librarian of the Royal Society, London; Jenny McCarthy; The Imperial War Museum; Monica Willan, L.T.B. Guide; Mrs Gray of Warrington Museum and Art Gallery; *Jewish Chronicle*; John E. Little of Uffington, Oxfordshire; Rosemary Treble; Penny Ward of the Central Library, Margate; Mrs K. East of the British Museum; Rev. W. G. Howells of Modbury in Devon; St Mary's College, Strawberry Hill; The British Federation of University Women, Frank Pynn, and Westminster Abbey.

Also to the staff of all the cemeteries, libraries, churches and hospitals who answered our questions with such patience and friendly interest.

Oxford University Press for permission to quote the Clerihew on Dame Laura Knight.

David Higham Associates Ltd, for permission to quote from *Finishing Touches* by Augustus John (Jonathan Cape, 1964).

The *Observer* for permission to quote the poem about Charley's Aunt by C. A. Lejeune.

FRANCES ABINGTON

1737–1815
(née Barton)
Cockspur St, SW1;
Drury Lane Theatre;
Eaton Square

Mrs Cibber, Peg Woffington, Mrs Yates, Kitty Clive and Mrs Abington were some of the temperamental, entrancing, infuriating and talented actresses of the eighteenth century. Frances Abington was born in London. Her father ran a cobbler's stall near Piccadilly, her brother was a stable-hand and worked just up the road. Fanny ran errands for pocket-money and then found a job taking messages for a French milliner in Cockspur Street. She also, at one time, sold flowers in the street, earning herself the nickname 'Nosegay Fan', and a reputation as a girl with an eye for the lads. If *The Secret History of the green Rooms* (1790) is to be believed: 'Her amours at this time were followed by a disagreeable consequence.'

When the 'consequence' had been cured, she found herself without money and without work, but a brothel owner, Sal Parker, befriended her and made her her personal maid and companion. Unfortunately Sal's protector took a fancy to Fanny and she was promptly fired.

Frances Abington probably first appeared on the stage at the Haymarket Theatre in a play called *The Busy Body* in 1752. She then moved on to Drury Lane.

During an intensive course of self-education she married her music teacher, Mr Abington. However, never having allowed anything to cramp her style, she proceeded to equal her success on stage with her success in bed:

> Conversant in amours, she now resolved to separate her lovers into two different classes: the first those whose liberality might enable her to live in splendour; and the second, those whom her humour pitched upon. For this purpose she had various houses in town for her various admirers. (*The Secret History of the Green Rooms*, 1790)

In 1782 she quarrelled with the management of Drury Lane and moved to Covent Garden. Mrs Abington continued to work well into her sixties; although in 1807 she was living in Eaton Square, her burial place is unknown.

DAME LOUISA ALDRICH-BLAKE

1865–1925
Bust: Tavistock Square, WC1

In a corner of Tavistock Square Gardens, London, there is an unusual double-sided monument to this woman of great integrity, who devoted her life to medicine. Making a speech to medical

Portrait of Louisa Brandreth Aldrich-Blake in Elizabeth Garrett Anderson Hospital, NW1

students she once said:

> Intellect and character, there are the two great influences which we bring to bear on the work which we do through life; and of the two, those who have had the best opportunity of judging, in the medical profession at any rate, consider that the influence of character on the career is the greater.

In 1893, already a doctor, Louisa Aldrich-Blake took the Bachelorship of Surgery, all the other candidates being men. She won first class Honours, qualified for the Gold Medal and later became the first woman to gain the degree of Master of Surgery. Her first post was at the Royal Free Hospital; she then became surgeon to the Elizabeth Garrett Anderson Hospital and, in 1914, was appointed Dean of the London School of Medicine for Women. Photographs and portraits of her reveal a strong face and a steady gaze, although she was described as having 'retained the manner of an attractive and almost painfully shy child'.

She was born at Welsh Bicknor on the Wye, Herefordshire; her ashes were returned there after her death.

ELIZABETH GARRETT ANDERSON

1836–1917
(née Garrett)
Elizabeth Garrett
Anderson Hospital,
144 Euston Road,
NW1;
Plaque: 20 Upper
Berkeley Street, W1

The Elizabeth Garrett Anderson Hospital in Euston Road, having defeated attempts to close it in the 1970s, now bustles with plans for extensive rebuilding. It is the direct descendant of a dispensary for women and children opened by Elizabeth Garrett after gaining her Certificate of the Society of Apothecaries in 1865.

Astounding her family by announcing, at the age of twenty, her decision to become a doctor, Elizabeth was in her early thirties before she gained her MD – in Paris. All her efforts in London had been frustrated. She started as a probationer-nurse at the Middlesex Hospital, but when allowed to attend some lectures and enter the dissecting-room, the other (male) students protested and she was barred. Later, by a majority of one, the Senate of

London University refused her application to be examined for matriculation. However, having finally opened the gates that had been, as her sister Millicent Garrett Fawcett said, '. . . not only closed, but barred, banged and bolted against women', the British Medical Association elected her a member in 1872.

Married to James Anderson, and having three children, Elizabeth worked until her retirement. She spent more and more time in Aldeburgh in Suffolk (her birthplace), was twice elected Mayor there and is buried in Aldeburgh churchyard.

QUEEN ANNE
1665–1714
Statues: outside St Paul's
Cathedral EC4;
Queen Anne's Gate, SW1

Outside St Paul's
Cathedral
  Brandy Nan
  Left in the lurch
  Face to the gin shops,
  Back to the church.
    Old London rhyme

A stony stare at Queen Anne's Gate, SW1

Poor Queen Anne! She had seventeen, or possibly eighteen, children, none of whom survived her, quarrelled bitterly with her closest friend Sarah, Duchess of Marlborough, and became enormously fat. She also seems to have been the only person who did not find her husband George, Prince of Denmark, an unutterable bore.

However, during her reign, prose and poetry sparkled with a razor-sharp elegance, architecture flourished and a delicate wild flower was christened 'Queen Anne's Lace'. She was buried in Westminster Abbey, and a copy of the original statue of her stands in front of St Paul's Cathedral. A less well-known statue of her can be found in Queen Anne's Gate, near St James's Park.

ANNE ASKEW
1521–1546
Tried: at the Guildhall, EC2 (Plaque);
Executed: near St Bartholomew-the-Great, West Smithfield, EC1

Burned outside St Bartholomew-the-Great, Smithfield in 1546

The Askews were an old Lancashire family. Anne developed an interest in religious disputation from an early age. When she embraced the Protestant faith her husband, Thomas Kyme, a Catholic, threw her out and she went to London. Soon known as a militant religious reformer, she was examined for heresy in 1545 – mainly for her refusal to accept the sacrament as the actual 'flesh, blood and bone' of Christ – but was released. On the next occasion, Anne told the examining council that 'it was a great shame for them to counsel contrary to their knowledge'. They sent her to Newgate prison. Further efforts to persuade her to abandon her beliefs failed completely and she was taken to the Tower of London.

5

Anne Askew contd.

The whole issue now became political. Members of the council hoped to force her into implicating certain people at court, particularly the Queen, Katherine Parr (q.v.). Brutally tortured (the rack finally being worked, quite illegally, by Lord Chancellor Wriothesley and Sir Richard Rich), her joints distorted and unable to stand, Anne still obstinately argued with them lying on the bare floor.

She was tried at the Guildhall (listed on a memorial of important trials in the Great Hall there) and condemned to be burnt at Smithfield. Carried there in a chair and tied to the stake, with a chain round her waist to support her, Anne criticised the sermon

preached before the execution by Dr Shaxton! When offered the King's pardon if she would recant she replied, 'I have not come hither to deny my master.'

Anne's name was not included on the 1870 memorial to the martyrs of Smithfield inscribed on the wall of St Bartholomew's Hospital.

PRINCESS SERAPHINE ASTAFIEVA

1876–1934
Plaque: 'The Pheasantry', 152 King's Road, Chelsea SW3

Princess Astafieva was tallish, aged about sixty, worldly and elegant, with slender legs and an indefinable mixture of the stylish and the slightly grubby that only such an aristocratic personality from Czarist Russia could hope to carry off successfully. She always wore a scarf tied turban-wise round her head, and carried a long cigarette holder. (Margot Fonteyn, *Autobiography*)

The daughter of a Russian prince, and the grand-niece of Count Tolstoy, Princess Astafieva was born in St Petersburg (now Leningrad) and studied at the Imperial Ballet School there. In 1895 she became a member of the Maryinski Ballet and, in 1896, married Josef Kshessinsky, a well-known character dancer. She stayed with the Maryinski for nearly ten years before leaving to join Diaghilev's Company. She

became one of his leading dancers, travelled the world and was singled out for her performance in Diaghilev's production of Fokine's 'Cleopatra'.

In 1914 she settled in London and began to teach: 152 King's Road in Chelsea became her home and her studio. It was there that Astafieva trained, among others, Anton Dolin, Alicia Markova and, for a brief period, Margot Fonteyn.

MARY ASTELL

1668–1731
Plaque: Chelsea Old Church (All Saints) Chelsea Embankment, SW3

Mary arrived in London in her twenties and lived there (mainly in Paradise Row, Chelsea) for the rest of her life. She wrote *A Serious Proposal to the Ladies*, suggesting the foundation of an education 'retreat' for women unable or unwilling to marry. Although she made it quite clear that this seminary would be run on Church of England principles, the idea was

nevertheless attacked as being 'Popish' and dangerous. An 'anonymous Lady' was persuaded to withdraw the offer of a large sum of money towards the project and the *Tatler* published a savage satire on the subject.

Undeterred, Mary continued to write and argue. A neighbour, Dr Atterbury, although he admired some of her opinions, was irritated

Home and studio of Princess Seraphine Astafieva, 152 King's Road, Chelsea, SW3

In abiding Memory of four Chelsea Women
distinguished by their learning and piety

who worshipped in this Church

MARGARET ROPER 1505-1544
Beloved daughter of Sir Thomas More

MAGDALEN HERBERT Lady Danvers
1568-1627 Mother of the Poet of The Temple

MARY ASTELL 1668-1731 Author of
The Serious Proposal to the Ladies

ELIZABETH BLACKWELL fl·1737
Compiler of The Curious Herbal

This tablet is dedicated by University Women of
Crosby Hall & by members of The Chelsea Society

by her blunt delivery and wrote to a friend:

> Had she as much good breeding as good sense, she would be perfect; but she has not the most decent manner of insinuating what she means, but is now and then a little offensive and shocking in her expressions.

The indomitable Miss Astell then became involved in the successful founding of a school for the daughters of Chelsea Pensioners. Towards the end of her life, she ordered a coffin and shroud to be made and brought to her bedside so that she could contemplate approaching death. She was buried at Chelsea (exact site unknown) and her name is on a plaque in Chelsea Old Church, placed there by the Federation of University Women to commemorate distinguished women of the area.

KATHERINE ASTLEY (or ASHLEY)
d. 1565
(née Champernowne)
Old Ludgate (Fleet)
Prison, Ludgate Hill, EC4

In 1537 Katherine Champernowne was appointed governess to the young and motherless Princess Elizabeth, second daughter of Henry VIII. Katherine, or 'Kat', as Elizabeth called her, was her tutor and friend for almost thirty years, and their relationship was one of great trust and affection.

Elizabeth's mother, Anne Boleyn, had been executed the year before and Elizabeth was four years old when Kat began to supervise her education. Later, Roger Ascham, her tutor, wrote to acknowledge the success of Kat's methods:

> Gentle Mrs Astley
> Would God my wit wist words would express the thanks you have deserved of all true English hearts,

for that noble imp (Elizabeth) by your labour and wisdom.

In 1545, Kat married John Astley, a cousin of Anne Boleyn's. Four years later an awkward situation occurred when Admiral Sir Thomas Seymour (Katherine Parr's (q.v.) husband) began to take too great an interest in the sixteen-year-old princess. Kat disapproved and said so, but was overruled. However, she found it difficult to be discreet and the gossip continued. Kat was taken away for questioning and threatened with dismissal. Elizabeth, although in an embarrassing situation, still flew to her friend's defence.

The 'noble imp' and the governess remained together through many troubled and often dangerous times and, when Elizabeth became queen, she immediately made her old friend Chief Lady of the Bedchamber. Seven years later the Spanish Ambassador to the English court, writing to the King of Spain, included a small item of news:

> On the 18th, Mistress Ashley, the Queen's governess died. Her Majesty went to see her the day before, and I am told she is greatly grieved.

NANCY, LADY ASTOR

1879–1964
(née Langhorne)
Married: All Souls' Church, Langham Place, W1;
London Home: 4 St James's Square, SW1

I do not begin by craving the indulgence of the House, for I am only too conscious of the indulgence and courtesy of the House. I knew it was very difficult for some of the Hon. members to receive the first lady MP into the House. It was almost as difficult for some as for the first lady MP to come in. (Opening remarks of Lady Astor's maiden speech in the House of Commons)

Nancy Astor was the first woman to sit in the House of Commons at Westminster. Born in Danville, Virginia, USA, she married Robert Gould Shaw II in 1897 and a year later gave birth to Robert Gould Shaw III. The marriage had very quickly shown signs of severe strain and in 1901 a deed of separation was signed. Two years after this the Shaws were divorced and Nancy left for Europe.

She loved England and spent a great deal of time there, finally marrying Waldorf Astor in 1906. They lived at Cliveden, near Maidenhead, Berkshire and, when in London, at 4 St James's Square. They had three children.

Waldorf Astor became MP for Plymouth in 1910 but, on the death of his father (the first Viscount Astor) in 1919, he was raised to the peerage and had to resign the seat. Nancy stood in his place and in November 1919 she became MP for the Sutton Division of Plymouth, a seat she held through six general elections. When her husband suggested that she should retire in 1944 she acquiesced, but the decision made her bitterly unhappy.

Nancy Astor was a convert to Christian Science and a strong supporter of the Temperance Movement (she introduced the Intoxicating Liquor – sale to persons under eighteen – Bill) but took no active part in the Suffrage Movement although it is said that she admired its aims. She could be tactless, obstinate, insensitive and impatient (a friend once told her that if she would only stop for a moment and think, she could be the greatest woman in England) but she fought for her convictions with courage, honesty, incredible vitality and a great sense of humour. Just after her death Lord Attlee wrote:

> People like Nancy Astor, quite apart from their good works, are atmospheric. They make things hum. One does not see many people of her calibre in public life today, which is a pity.

Her ashes were buried, with her husband's, in the eighteenth-century Octagon Temple in the grounds at Cliveden.

Nancy Astor: Her home at 4 St James's Square, SW1

JANE AUSTEN

1775–1817
Henrietta Street, WC2;
Plaque: Poets' Corner,
Westminster Abbey;
Also Plaque: 23 Hans
Place, SW1

Single Women have a dreadful propensity for being poor – which is one very strong argument in favour of Matrimony.

Hampshire born, with connections in Bath, Jane (unmarried) was buried in Winchester Cathedral. Her calm little ghost may be traced to London, where she stayed with her favourite brother, Henry, at his homes in Sloane Street, Henrietta Street and Hans Place, visiting her publishers, Thomas Egerton of Whitehall and later John Murray in Albemarle Street.

Never a prolific writer, she produced only six novels, of which *Pride and Prejudice*, *Emma*, *Mansfield Park* and the delightful satire on Gothic novelists, *Northanger Abbey*, entitle her to her place among the greatest writers of English fiction.

JOANNA BAILLIE

1762–1851
Buried: St John's Church,
Church Row, Hampstead,
NW3;
Plaque: Bolton House,
Windmill Hill, NW3

Joanna was a poet and a playwright. Although born in Lanarkshire, Scotland, she lived in London for more than sixty years, over forty of them in Hampstead:

> It is a goodly sight through the clear air,
> From Hampstead's heathy height to see at once
> England's vast capital in fair expanse,
> Towers, belfries, lengthen'd streets and structures fair

Perhaps the most interesting idea she had was to take various human 'passions' and to present each one both as a tragedy and a comedy. When produced on stage, however, the experiment seems to have failed:

Went to the theatre in the evening, to see Mrs Baillie's *De Montford*, which went off very heavily. One is at first amazed that what reads so well, should act so ill. (*The Gentleman's Magazine*, 1835)

Among her many friends and admirers were Mary Somerville, Maria Edgeworth and Sir Walter Scott, with whom she corresponded regularly. She was buried in Hampstead Parish Church (St John's) and her grave is still to be seen in the churchyard there.

Her home – Bolton House, Hampstead

LADY BANCROFT

1839–1921
(née Marie Wilton)
Theatre Royal,
Haymarket, SW1;
Brompton Cemetery,
SW6

An actor's daughter, Marie Wilton became a star of burlesque; borrowed money; acquired an old theatre and, as manager, ran it very efficiently. After her marriage to Squire Bancroft, they took over the Haymarket and it was here, in 1881, that they offered Lillie Langtry (q.v.) her first opportunity to appear on the professional stage. Marie's husband was later knighted.

Sir Squire and Lady Bancroft were buried in Brompton Cemetery. A bomb destroyed the tomb during the Second World War, but an inscribed stone still lies on the ground there. Above their names are the words: 'From shadows and fancies to the truth.'

ANN LAETITIA BARBAULD

1743–1825
(née Aikin)
Lived: Church Row,
Hampstead, NW3;
Buried: Abney Park
Cemetery, Stoke
Newington, N16

Concerning a Marble
And with reference to the game of
Taw beloved by Schoolboys

The world's something bigger
But just of this figure
And speckled with mountains and
seas;
Your heroes are overgrown
schoolboys
Who scuffle for empires and toys,
And kick the poor ball as they
please.
Now Caesar, now Pompey, gives
law;
And Pharsalia's plain,
Though heaped with the slain,
Was only a game at *Taw*.

Anna Aikin had already published a volume of poetry, *Miscellaneous Poems, Chiefly Lyrical*, before her marriage to Rochemont Barbauld, a nonconformist minister. She helped her husband to run a school at Palgrave, in Suffolk, after which they travelled abroad and, on their return, lived in Church Row, Hampstead.

Mrs Barbauld wrote stories for children, hymns, poetry and also some political pamphlets of a radical nature. Horace Walpole disliked her and called her 'the Virago Barbauld'.

Her husband suffered from mental illness and they moved to Stoke Newington, where she continued to live after his death. She was buried there in Abney Park Cemetery.

DR 'JAMES MIRANDA BARRY'

c. 1799–1865
Buried: Kensal Green
Cemetery, NW10

In 1865, Inspector-General Dr 'James Barry' died in London, having served as a physician and surgeon in the British Army for almost forty-six years. An Irish woman, Sophia Blake, who laid out the body was shocked into protest . . . this was not a man's body she had dealt with, but a woman's.

Over a hundred years later, the mystery has still not been entirely solved, although June Rose, in her careful, well-documented study *The Perfect Gentleman* (1977) paints a brilliant and fascinating portrait of a woman who successfully remained 'a man' throughout her life. Dressed as a boy, and with Lord Buchan, the artist James Barry RA and the South American, General Miranda, as patrons, 'James Barry' enrolled at Edinburgh University and qualified as a doctor. He then became a Pupil Dresser at St Thomas's Hospital in London and, in 1813, enlisted in the army.

Posted to the Cape as an Assistant Surgeon to the Forces, Dr James Barry soon became physician to the Governor, Lord Charles Somerset, and his daughters. He soon gained a reputation as an excellent doctor and an enthusiastic reformer.

There were jokes and innuendoes about his relationship with the Governor and Barry finally resigned. In 1827 he was made an Army Staff Surgeon and moved to Mauritius, then Jamaica, St Helena and Antigua. Although sometimes touchy, reserved and bad-tempered, it was noticed that Dr Barry improved the standard of medical treatment wherever he went.

His last post, as Inspector-General, was in Canada, but in 1859, weakened by influenza, he returned to England and was, reluctantly, retired. After a few years of some rather aimless travel he went back to London, fell ill and died.

ANN CHARLOTTE BARTHOLO-MEW

1800–1862
(née Fayermann)
Buried: Highgate Cemetery (West), Swains Lane, N6

Born at Lodden, Norfolk, Ann Fayerman spent most of her life in London. Before her first marriage to Walter Turnbull she had already done some successful writing; her farce *It's Only My Aunt* was published in 1825. After her marriage she took up painting, specialising in miniatures, and continued to write. Widowed, she then married Valentine Bartholomew (flower painter to Queen Victoria), who encouraged her to try painting flowers too, which she proceeded to do exquisitely. Her work was frequently exhibited.

Although delicate in health, she worked extremely hard. Writing about her in *English Female Artists* (1876), Miss Clayton remarked: 'Devoted as she was for many years to her profession the *Artist* never forgot the duties of a *Woman*.'!

ADELAIDE BARTLETT

1856–?
(née de la Tremouille)
Claverton Street, Pimlico, SW1 (No. 85 no longer exists)

Adelaide Bartlett's origins remain a mystery. Although she was brought up by nuns at a convent in France, she is supposed to have been the unacknowledged daughter of an Englishman of good social position. Her marriage (at Croydon in 1875) to Edwin Bartlett, Family Grocer, is thought to have been 'arranged' by her unknown father. She and her husband moved to Merton, Surrey, Adelaide gave birth to a stillborn baby and Edwin made a will leaving everything to her.

It was in Merton that she met the Reverend George Dyson. Not only was she greatly attracted to him but Edwin, rather strangely, seems to have encouraged their relationship. In 1885 after a holiday in Dover, Adelaide took lodgings at 85 Claverton Street, Pimlico, and moved in with her husband. George Dyson was a frequent visitor. Edwin Bartlett then became ill, suffering from a strange variety of symptoms, from nausea and exhaustion to depression and insomnia. Three months after they had moved to Claverton Street he was dead.

In April 1866, after an inquest, both Adelaide Bartlett and George Dyson were sent for trial at the Old Bailey. That Edwin had been poisoned was obvious, that George Dyson had bought five ounces of chloroform and given it to Adelaide was established, but no evidence was offered against Dyson. No one seemed able to prove how Adelaide could have administered the liquid chloroform. Brilliantly defended by Sir Edward Clarke KC, she was acquitted.

After the trial, the consulting surgeon of St Bartholomew's Hospital remarked that now it was all over, 'she should tell us in the interests of science how she did it.' Adelaide did not oblige, but vanished, taking her secret with her. Later it was discovered that she lived in America for some time and may have died there, but the date of her death is unknown.

ELIZABETH BARTON

1506–1534
Christchurch, Newgate Street, EC1 (Churchyard barely exists)

Recovering from a severe illness, Elizabeth, servant of Thomas Cobb of Aldington, Kent, began to hear voices, go into trances and make prophecies of a simple religious nature. The parish priest, convinced that she was inspired by the Holy Ghost, sent a report to Archbishop Warham and two monks arrived to investigate. One of them, Edward Bocking, quickly realised her potential in the disturbed religious climate of the time. Having painstakingly trained her in detailed doctrine and propaganda, he encouraged the trances and 'prophecies' and, with voices apparently coming from her belly and publicised as 'miracles', Elizabeth was regarded with some awe. She became known as 'The Nun of Kent'. Once, in the king's presence, she prophesied doom to Henry VIII and his marriage to Anne Boleyn (q.v.).

Arrested in 1533, she was brought to London before Archbishop Cranmer. Pleading innocence, and exploitation by clever men, she was temporarily pardoned, but in 1534 she was hanged at Tyburn, London, and buried in the churchyard of Grey Friars, Newgate (now called Christchurch, Newgate Street).

LILIAN BAYLIS

1874–1937
Lived: Stockwell Park Road, SW9;
Plaque: St Paul's, Covent Garden

Traditionally, St Paul's, Covent Garden is the 'actor's church'. Inside, at the back of the church, there are rows of memorial plaques, all dedicated to well-known theatrical personalities. One of them reads:

> Lilian Baylis
> 9 May 1874   25 November 1937
> Old Vic   Sadlers Wells
> Lessee and Manager of both
>   theatres
> 'Thou thy worldly task hast done,
> Home art gone . . .'
>   (*Cymbeline* Act IV Scene II)

Miss Baylis took over the management of the Old Vic after the death of her aunt, Emma Cons (q.v.), in 1912. She turned it into the home of Shakespeare and of opera in English with little money but with single-minded devotion and, as far as she was concerned, the direct help of God. She was also responsible for the re-opening of Sadlers Wells Theatre in 1931.

She lived for many years at 27 Stockwell Park Road and when she died her ashes were scattered in the East London Cemetery. She had asked that there be no grave or memorial.

DOROTHEA BEALE

1831–1906
Queen's College,
43 Harley Street, W1

> Said Miss Beale to Miss Buss
> 'There is no one like us.'
> Said Miss Buss to Miss Beale,
> 'That is just what I feel.'

Dorothea Beale taught in London at the school which was part of Queen's College, Harley Street, for seven years. She was engaged to be married, but the engagement was broken off, and she accepted a position as Head Teacher at the Clergy Daughters School in Casterton. Unable to agree with the methods of teaching there, she was dismissed within a year.

In 1858 she applied for the vacancy as Head of Cheltenham Ladies College and was appointed. The school – for upper-class girls, no tradesmen's daughters need apply – was in grave danger of closure. Miss Beale not only saved it but devoted the rest of her life to her Ladies College in particular and to the education of girls in general.

MARY BEALE

1632/3–1699
(née Cradock)

Buried: St James's,
Piccadilly, SW1 (grave not
marked)

Born in Suffolk, Mary married
Charles Beale when she was
nineteen. They eventually moved
to London, living at first in the
Covent Garden area and then in
Hind Court, just off Fleet Street,
where Mary, already an
enthusiastic artist, set up her own
studio.

By the time they moved to a new
house in Pall Mall she was ready to
become a professional, and
successful, portrait painter.

Influenced by her friend and
adviser, Sir Peter Lely (who
became chief painter to the court
of Charles II), Mary was able to
support her family by her work.
She also took on pupils and trained
her son, Charles. Her early and
accomplished self-portrait was
bought by the trustees of the
National Portrait Gallery in 1912.

St James's Church,
Piccadilly

LADY MARGARET BEAUFORT

**c. 1441–1509
(Countess of Richmond and Derby)**
Tomb: Henry VII Chapel, Westminster Abbey, (South Aisle), SW1

Three hundred and sixty-nine years after her death, Lady Margaret Beaufort was adopted as patroness of a new women's college at Oxford, Lady Margaret Hall. One assumes that she would have been delighted, as she had been involved in the foundation of Christ's College and St John's College, Cambridge during her lifetime.

She had walked the tightrope of politics, married three times and had given birth to a son ('my dear heart', as she called him) who became Henry VII. In middle age, while running the domestic affairs of her son's court, she was able to indulge her interest in books, religious reform and the new art of printing. William Caxton set up his press at Westminster under her patronage and Wynkyn de Worde styled himself 'Prynter unto the moost excellent pryncesse my lady the kynges moder'.

Lady Margaret died in London, having attended the coronation of her grandson, Henry VIII, and was, as she had wished, buried in Westminster Abbey. On her tomb, in the cramped south aisle of the Henry VII chapel, is a beautiful effigy executed by Pietro Torrigiano.

ISABELLA BEETON

**1836–1865
(née Mayson)**
Born: Milk Street, EC2; Buried: Norwood (South Metropolitan) Cemetery, Norwood High Street, SE27

In 1948, in spite of bomb damage, Milk Street in the City of London was still recognisably the place where 'Mrs Beeton' was born. Today it is just another narrow street lined with bleakly impersonal offices and Number 24, her birthplace, has vanished.

Intelligent, practical and energetic, Isabella died, aged only twenty-eight, of puerperal fever after the birth of her fourth child. She was buried in Norwood Cemetery, but her real memorial is *Beeton's Book of Household Management*, first published in volume form by her husband Samuel in 1861. It had taken her four years to complete and made her name a household word for over a century. She had hoped for a large family but her first two children both died, one at three months, the other at three years old. Before her own tragic death she had completed her *Dictionary of Cooking* and to it her husband added his own sad farewell, ending:

> This memory, this presence, will nerve the father, left alone, to continue to do his duty; in which he will follow the example of his wife, for her duty no woman has ever better accomplished than the late Isabella Mary Beeton.

Buried in Norwood Cemetery beneath the brambles

APHRA BEHN

1640–1689
(née Amis)
Buried: Westminster
Abbey Cloisters, (East
Walk) SW1

**Buried in the cloisters of
Westminster Abbey are
Aphra Behn and Ann
Bracegirdle**

The background of the first woman in England actually to earn her living by writing is obscure. She seems to have spent her early years in Surinam, but, returning to England, she married a merchant of the City of London and became a popular visitor at the court of Charles II. By 1666 she was a merry widow. When war against the Dutch broke out, she was sent to Antwerp as a spy and learned that the Dutch fleet was planning a surprise visit up the Thames. Aphra informed London, but was not believed – the Dutch proved her right!

Aphra Behn became a professional and prolific writer. She knew Dryden, Otway and Southerne and her plays were among the most successful of the Restoration theatre. One of them, *The Feigned Courtezans*, she dedicated to Nell Gwynn (q.v.). It is remarkable that none of her plays has been recently produced.

Visitors walk over her grave in Westminster Abbey and the inscription is faint:

> Mrs Aphra Behn
> Dyed April 16 AD 1689
> Here lies a proof that wit can never be
> Defence enough against mortality

GERTRUDE BELL

1868–1926
Educated: Queen's
College, 43 Harley Street,
W1

We inclined right, over flats of limestone and sand, and saw a distant corner of the Great Nefudh, the famous belts of sand-dune which cut off Jebel Shammar from the Syrian Desert. Palgrave, the Blunts, and Gertrude Bell among the storied travellers had crossed it. (*Seven Pillars of Wisdom*, T. E. Lawrence)

Born in Durham, educated at Queen's College, Harley Street, London, and at Lady Margaret Hall, Oxford, Gertrude Bell became a respected explorer and a brilliant linguist. She first visited Teheran in Persia with relatives, studied Persian and there fell in love with Henry Cadogan. They decided to become engaged but, while she was away in England, he caught a chill and died. Desperately unhappy, Gertrude continued to travel and also began mountain-climbing. She seemed to enjoy courting danger.

By 1899 she was living in Jerusalem, where she learnt Arabic and made her first journey through the desert. During the First World War she worked for the Red Cross, tracing the 'missing and wounded', but was later sent to Cairo, where she joined the Arab Intelligence Bureau and compiled a tribal register.

In 1919 she attended the Peace Conference in Paris, with Prince Faisal and T. E. Lawrence (Lawrence of Arabia). After a short rest, she returned to Baghdad, where she became President of the Salam Library and also helped to create the Baghdad Museum.

Gertrude Bell died suddenly in Baghdad, and was buried with full military honours in the cemetery outside the city. A tablet was erected in the museum to her 'whose memory the Arabs will ever hold in reverence and affection'

VANESSA BELL

1879–1961
(née Stephen)
Lived: 46 Gordon Square,
WC1

Vanessa Bell, sister of Virginia Woolf (q.v.), was born in London. She studied art under Sir Arthur Cope RA and, from 1901 to 1904, attended the Royal Academy Schools.

In 1907 she married Clive Bell, writer and critic. They lived at 46 Gordon Square, which had been the home of the Stephen children for the previous three years and had seen the founding of the 'Bloomsbury Group'. A year later she gave birth to Julian, the first of her three children.

Influenced at first by the work of Whistler and Sargent, Vanessa then met Roger Fry, artist and critic, with whom she later had an affair, and became one of the directors of his 'Omega Workshop' in Fitzroy Square. Inspired by her experiments in design there, and by the excitement of the Post-Impressionist exhibitions held in London, she gradually changed her style, developing into a superb colourist and working on the problems of form and visual expression.

In 1916 she moved to

Charleston, Firle, near Lewes in Sussex, which was to be her home for the rest of her life, and where she and her lover Duncan Grant, the artist, began the unique decoration of the farmhouse.

Vanessa Bell continued to travel extensively, to paint, exhibit and entertain. She designed all the dust-jackets for Virginia's books and taught in 1938 at the Euston Road School (founded by a group of English artists). She died at Charleston and was buried at Firle. A very beautiful woman, she seems to have had a strong, serene personality which was described by her daughter:

> She sat and sewed or painted or listened; she was always sitting, sometimes at the head of the table, sometimes by the fire, sometimes under the apple tree. Even if she said little, there emanated from her an enormous power, a pungency like the smell of crushed sage.
> (From *Recollections of Virginia Woolf*, ed. Joan Russell Noble)

ANNIE BESANT

1847–1933
(née Wood)
Plaque: 39 Colby Road,
SE19

Rebel, writer, free-thinker, socialist, orator, Theosophist, Annie Besant was a versatile and astonishing woman. She was born in London; her father died when she was five and her mother, moving the family to Harrow, ran a boarding-house for boys of Harrow School. Annie was sent to a boarding-school in Dorset, and became almost obsessively 'religious'. At the age of eighteen, while visiting an aunt who lived in Chelsea, she attended the local church and met the young vicar, Frank Besant. She became his devoted admirer, but when he misunderstood her approach and assumed they would marry, she was considerably shaken. Only when her mother showed disapproval did Annie decide that she *must* marry him – and did so in 1867.

It was a disaster. She soon became bored, restless and disillusioned. Giving birth to two children, a boy and a girl, solved few of her problems and Annie began to write short stories and religious pamphlets. Frank Besant imagined that 'discipline' was the answer . . . he was wrong. In 1873 his wife went home to her mother and refused to return. A separation was arranged. Annie took a job as a governess but, after her mother's death, was attracted to the ideas of the National Secular Society, the Free-Thinkers, and their leader, Charles Bradlaugh, with whom she was to have a long, affectionate

relationship. She threw herself into their cause with enthusiasm and gained a reputation as a brilliant orator. Later, at odds with the Free-Thinkers, she began to attend the meetings of the New Socialists and Fabians. One evening, having listened to Bernard Shaw speak, she rose at the end of the meeting and (to Shaw's astonishment) supported his ideas. From that time she threw all her energy into Socialist causes, founding a new paper called *The Link* in which she took up, amongst other causes, that of the striking Bryant and May match-girls.

Then, in 1889, Annie Besant became a Theosophist, visiting India for the first time in 1893. There she later founded the Central Hindu College and also became involved in the Home Rule for India issue:

> I am old, but I believe that I shall see Home Rule before I die. If I have helped ever so little to the realization of that glorious hope I am satisfied. Varde Mataram. God save India.

She was imprisoned, and after her release was elected President of the Indian National Congress. In 1924 a meeting (which she attended), was held in her honour at the Queen's Hall in London. Annie died at Adyar, Madras, in India. Some of her ashes were scattered on the River Ganges, the rest were placed in a garden of remembrance at Adyar.

ELIZABETH BILLINGTON

1768–1818
Leicester Square, WC2;
Covent Garden, WC2

Elizabeth came from a musical family and was a very talented child. She had composed two piano sonatas before she was twelve and then began to develop a fine singing voice. She became known as 'England's Greatest Singer'.

In 1783 she married James Billington, a double bass player, at Lambeth Church in London. They went to Dublin where she made her debut as Polly Peachum in *The Beggar's Opera*. Returning to

London she sang at Covent Garden and was such an outstanding success that she was retained for the whole season and paid £1,000. Sir Joshua Reynolds painted her as St Cecilia and she is said to have had a torrid affair with the Prince of Wales (later Geroge IV).

In 1794 Elizabeth left England with her husband. In Naples she met Sir William Hamilton and his wife Emma (q.v.), and was persuaded to sing at the Teatro San Carlo. Then her husband died suddenly and for a while she toured Italy, accompanied by her brother, singing in most of the principal cities. In 1799 she married for the second time, but soon discovered that her new husband, a young Frenchman called Felissent, indulged in wife-beating. Two years later she managed to return to England without him and, in October 1801, appeared in Thomas Arne's *Artaxerxes* at Covent Garden. She was given a tumultuous welcome by a public delighted to see her back.

M. Felissent followed his wife to London, but was quickly arrested and deported as an alien. Elizabeth remained and continued singing successfully until her retirement. She lived for a while in Fulham and then, in 1817, returned to Italy where she owned property near Venice. Her husband joined her there. She died the following year after receiving a severe blow on the head.

DR ELIZABETH BLACKWELL

1821–1910
Worked at St Bartholomew's Hospital, West Smithfield, EC1

Although Elizabeth was born in Bristol, her family emigrated and she was brought up and educated in America. She ran a school in Kentucky for a while and then decided that she would prefer to study medicine. After various difficulties she was offered a place at Geneva (northern New York State) where, in 1849, she gained her degree. So unusual was this achievement that it was commemorated in *Punch*:

> Young ladies all of every clime
> Especially of Britain,
> Who wholly occupy your time
> In novels or in knitting,
> Whose highest skill is but to play,
> Sing, dance, or French to clack well,
> Reflect on the example, pray,
> Of excellent Miss Blackwell.

An eye-infection, caught while working at La Maternité Hospital in Paris, eventually led to blindness in one eye and prevented her from becoming a surgeon. She returned to America, where she helped to found a hospital for women in New York, but finally settled in London. There she lectured, established a medical practice at 6 Burnwood Place and was appointed Professor of Gynaecology at the London School of Medicine.

In 1897 her health deteriorated and she moved to Hastings. For many years her favourite holiday resort had been Scotland and when she died she was buried at Kilmun on the shores of Holy Loch.

ELIZABETH BLACKWELL

d. 1758?
(Maiden name unknown)
Swan Walk and Chelsea Physic Garden, SW3; Plaque: Chelsea Old Church, SW3

To Isaac Rand Apothecary and Fellow of the Royal Society –
Sir
    Your Readiness to Assist and Instruct me in this Undertaking (which otherways would have been very imperfect) is so visible to every Judge, who must know that I had no skill in Botany, that I am under a Necessity to declare that it is to you I am obliged for every compleat Part of this Work and therefore I hope you will accept of this small Acknowledgment which Gratitude obliges me to make.

I am with the greatest Respect and Esteem
Sir your much obliged
Humble Servant
Elizabeth Blackwell
Chelsea August ye 16th 1737.

Elizabeth may have been born in Scotland but is also said to have been the daughter of a merchant of the City of London. She married Alexander Blackwell, who spent both her money and his on various schemes until he was imprisoned

Gateway to discovery leading into Chelsea Physic Garden from Swan Walk, SW3

for debt. Elizabeth came to his rescue. Having some artistic ability, and hearing that illustrations might be needed for a proposed *Herbal*, she approached Sir Hans Sloane (physician and benefactor) and showed him some of her work. He and his friends were impressed and encouraged her to continue.

Installed in a house in Swan Walk, bordering one side of the Chelsea Physic Garden, Elizabeth proceeded to draw, and tint, a large collection of the Garden's medical plants. *A Curious Herbal* (1737–39) contained 'five hundred cuts of the most useful Plants which are now used in the practice of Physick'.

In this way she paid for her husband's release. He then left hurriedly for Sweden where, for a while, he advised on agriculture and became the King's physician.

Elizabeth, still living in Chelsea, received an occasional allowance from him and intended to follow him to Sweden, but Alexander became involved in some dangerous political plotting there and was executed. She is said to have remained in Chelsea and to have died there in 1758.

CATHERINE BLAKE

c. 1762–1831
(née Boucher)
Lived: 17 South Molton Street (Plaque);
Buried: Bunhill Fields Cemetery, EC1

Edith Sitwell described her as 'the most wonderful wife who has ever comforted and supported a man of genius'. Daughter of a market-gardener, Catherine was illiterate when she married William Blake in 1782. By 1784 she could not only read and write but had become his assistant, learning all the delicate finishing techniques for his prints and engravings. Later she helped him throughout the production of his *Songs of Innocence*, finally stitching the loose papers into covers.

Catherine had to be an exceptionally careful housewife as they were always short of money. During a period of relative affluence they lived in Lambeth and were also able to rent a country cottage in Felpham, West Sussex. Catherine's delight shows in a letter she wrote to a friend: 'My husband has been obliged to finish several things before our migration; the swallows call us, fleeting past our window at this moment.'

After 1803, very poor again, they lived in South Molton Street, William still working and dreaming. Catherine wrote: 'I have very little of Mr Blake's company; he is always in Paradise.' When he died she worked for a while as a housekeeper and then moved into lodgings. Four years later, as she lay dying, Catherine called out to William that she would be with him very soon. They are buried together in Bunhill Fields cemetery (entrance off the City Road, opposite Wesley's Chapel).

NEAR BY LIE THE REMAINS OF
THE POET-PAINTER
WILLIAM BLAKE
1757 – 1827
AND OF HIS WIFE
CATHERINE SOPHIA
1762 – 1831

ANNE BOLEYN

1503?–1536

Executed and buried: The
Tower of London, EC3

Born at Blickling Hall in Norfolk (although more popularly associated with Hever Castle in Kent), Anne Boleyn is difficult to assess. Hemmed in by ambition and political intrigue, and probably the only wife that Henry VIII genuinely and passionately adored, she hovers, elusive and independent, refusing to reveal her secret self. Intelligent and vivacious, she enjoyed singing, dancing and hunting, loved dogs, loathed Cardinal Wolsey and gave birth to a daughter, Elizabeth. Unfortunately Anne overestimated her power over Henry and underestimated her enemies who, finally, ensured her downfall. Accused of adultery with several men and incest with her brother, she met her death in the Tower of London with dignity. During the expected speech, and minutes before the executioner severed her 'little neck', she said: 'I pray God to save the King, and send him long to reign over you, for a gentler nor a more merciful prince was there never . . .'

She was buried in the Tower church of St Peter ad Vincula, in an arrow box: they had neglected to order a coffin.

**St Peter ad Vincula,
Tower of London**

CATHERINE BOOTH

1829–1890
(née Mumford)
Buried: Abney Park
Cemetery, Stoke
Newington, N16

Catherine and William Booth founded the Salvation Army. Catherine edited their first magazine, the *East London Evangelist*, a small monthly paper that later developed into the well-known weekly, *The War Cry*. Totally supporting her husband, she accompanied him everywhere, preached herself, and concentrated particularly on the problems of women and children in the cities.

She also gave birth to eight children, five daughters and three sons.

When she died, her funeral service is said to have been attended by 36,000. Her last letter, addressed to the Army, ended:

> I send you my blessing. Fight on, and God will be with you. Victory comes at last. I will meet you in Heaven. Catherine Booth.

CATHERINE BOOTH-CLIBBORN

1858–1955
(née Booth)
Buried: Highgate
Cemetery (East), Swains
Lane, N6

Catherine, or Kate, as she was usually called, was a daughter of William and Catherine Booth, founders of the Salvation Army. Brought up in a background of praying, singing and preaching, she first spoke at an open air meeting in Hackney when she was fourteen. When the Salvation Army was properly launched in 1878, she was enlisted as one of their first women officers.

Kate showed her true mettle when, accompanied by Adelaide Cox and Florence Soper, she was sent on a mission to Paris. Living in appalling conditions, they visited areas where the police patrolled in pairs. They preached in the streets, were met with violence and abuse and often returned to their rooms bruised and bleeding. This only stiffened Kate's resolve and her brother Bramwell dubbed her 'La Maréchale'. It was in Paris that she met Arthur Clibborn for the first time – a Quaker who had arrived to join the Salvation Army in France.

In 1883 the battle was moved to Switzerland. Banned in Geneva, Kate held secret meetings and then helped to form a corps at Neuchâtel. Forbidden to speak there, she held a meeting five miles outside the town, was arrested and sent to jail. In England *Punch* launched into verse:

> Hey for our Catherine, blushing so feminine,
> Rousing the Swiss to conviction of sin;
> Out on the 'beak' who, the tide of grace stemmin', in
> Sisted on brutally running her in.

Acquitted, she finally returned to England where, in 1887, she married Arthur. They continued their work for the Salvation Army, although later her husband's pacifism caused problems and Kate decided that she could no longer remain under the Army's authority. She also broke with her family, a decision that caused her great unhappiness.

Well into her nineties when she died, she was buried beside her husband in Highgate Cemetery (East).

BOUDICCA

d. AD 61
Statue: Westminster
Bridge (North), SW1

She was very tall, in appearance terrifying, in the glance of her eye most fierce, and her voice was harsh; a great mass of the tawniest hair fell to her hips.

Thus Dio Cassius, in his *Roman History*, described Boudicca, Queen of the British tribe known as the Iceni.

In the winter of AD 59–60 Boudicca's husband, King Prasutagus, died. he had ruled his people well as a 'client-king'

appointed by the Roman conquerors. Now he had dutifully left half his wealth to the Emperor Nero and the rest to his two daughters. His wife, he may have assumed, would at least be treated fairly by the Romans, possibly even nominated as client-queen in his place. Instead, they plundered his household and kingdom, flogged his wife, raped his daughters and humiliated his tribe. This caused a rebellion that flared into a catastrophe of appalling magnitude. Led by Boudicca, the Iceni rose and, joined by some neighbouring tribes, began to move southwards. The Roman Governor and Commander-in-Chief, Suetonius Paulinus, with the Fourteenth and Twentieth Legions, was occupied elsewhere. Boudicca had the field virtually to herself.

> I am not fighting for my kingdom and wealth now. I am fighting as an ordinary person for my lost freedom, my bruised body, and my outraged daughters. (Tacitus, *Annals of Imperial Rome*)

Camulodunum, now Colchester, was the first place to feel the fury of the advancing hordes. It was sacked, savagely and bloodily. Then came the turn of Verulamium (St Alban's) and Londinium. Both cities soon lay in smoking ruins, their citizens – British as well as Romans – massacred in their thousands; Boudicca and her followers spared no one.

It is not known exactly where the Roman army finally came to grips with the British in AD 61, but it was a victory for the discipline and efficiency of the Roman troops and a total defeat for the British. Boudicca, it was rumoured, poisoned herself after the battle and the Iceni were wiped out.

Today Boudicca (as imagined by Thomas Thorneycroft in one of the most dramatic statues in London), erect on a war chariot, her daughters crouching by her side, storms relentlessly towards the Houses of Parliament at the north end of Westminster Bridge.

'She was very tall, in appearance terrifying, In the glance of her eye most fierce . . .'

HENRIETTA BOWDLER

1754–1830
No address traced so far

Dr Thomas Bowdler immortalised the family name by 'purifying' – or 'bowdlerising' – the works of Shakespeare. His sister, Henrietta, wrote poetry, essays and religious works, dividing most of her life between Bath and London. Her *Poems and Essays* was published in Bath in 1786 and her *Sermons on the Doctrines and Duties of Christianity*, published anonymously, so delighted Bishop Porteous of London that:

. . . under the idea of their having been written by a clergyman, he offered, through the publisher, to confer a living upon the author. *The Gentleman's Magazine*, 1830

Her autobiography *Pen Tamar; or the History of an Old Maid* was published posthumously.

ANNE BRACEGIRDLE

1663?–1748
Buried: Westminster Abbey Cloisters (East Walk)

As Colley Cibber remarked, Anne 'threw out such a glow of health and chearfulness (sic) that on the stage few spectators that were not past it could behold her without desire'.

Anne was Congreve's leading lady; she was also rumoured to have been his mistress. She created the role of Millamant in *The Way of the World*, but although her

stage career was spectacularly successful, it was rather short. She left the theatre for ever in 1707 because people said that Anne Oldfield (q.v.), a young rival, had played a favourite role better than she had!

Anne died aged eighty-five and was buried in the east walk of Westminster Abbey, close to Aphra Behn (q.v.).

MARY ELIZABETH BRADDON

1837–1915
(Mrs Maxwell)
Memorial: St Mary's Church, Richmond, Surrey

The same August sun which had gone down behind the waste of waters glimmered redly upon the broad face of the old clock over that ivy-covered archway which leads into the gardens of Audley Court.

A fierce and crimson sunset. The mullioned windows and twinkling lattices are all ablaze with the red glory; the fading light flickers upon the leaves of the limes in the long avenue, and changes the still fish-pond into a sheet of burnished copper; even into those dim recesses of brier and brushwood, amidst which the old well is hidden, the crimson brightness penetrates in fitful flashes till the dank weeds and the rusty iron wheel and broken woodwork seem as if they were flecked with blood. (*Lady Audley's Secret*)

An early thriller, Mary Braddon's *Lady Audley's Secret* published in 1862, was an immense success and earned Miss Braddon a great deal of money and a rather exaggerated reputation as a sensational writer.

Mary married John Maxwell, the publisher, in 1874, having lived with him for nearly fourteen years

and borne several children. She wrote plays, edited magazines, contributed to *Punch* and published a large number of novels, although *Lady Audley's Secret* is the best known.

Aged seventy-seven, she died at her home, Lichfield House in Richmond, and was buried in Richmond Parish Church, where there is a memorial to her:

A writer of rare and refined scholarship
Who gave profitable and pleasurable literature
To countless readers in her library of
Three score and ten works of fiction.

FANNY (FRANCES) BRAWNE

1800–1865
(Mrs Lindon)
Keats House, Keats
Grove, Hampstead, NW3

Fanny was engaged to the poet John Keats, and is remembered only for that reason. She and her mother lived next door to Armitage Brown and Keats in Hampstead and helped to nurse him before he went to Italy. The two houses now form the Keats Memorial House in Keats Grove.

The letters he wrote to Fanny were very emotional, often tormented and always beautiful: 'I will imagine you Venus tonight, and pray, pray, pray to your star like a heathen.' and: 'I wish to believe in immortality – I wish to live with you for ever.'

After Keats' death she married a Mr Louis Lindon. Her grave is in the Brompton Cemetery, West Kensington.

THE BRONTË SISTERS

Plaque: Poets' corner, Westminster Abbey; Door-panel: 32 Cornhill, EC3

The Brontë sisters, Charlotte, Emily and Anne, were an extraordinary phenomenon. Daughters of a country parson, they were brought up with their brother, Branwell, in the remote moorland village of Haworth in Yorkshire. In this isolated existence, the four children invented fantasy worlds and wrote about them in tiny handwriting. Branwell became a wastrel and a drunkard. His sisters all became novelists and wrote with a passionate realism that startled the novel-reading public of the time.

In October 1847, Charlotte's *Jane Eyre* was published and was a great success. In December the same year Anne's *Agnes Grey* and Emily's *Wuthering Heights* appeared but were relative failures. Emily died, aged thirty, the following year, unaware that

Wuthering Heights would one day be hailed as a work of undoubted genius. Anne and Charlotte continued to write but they too died young, Anne aged twenty-nine and Charlotte at thirty-nine.

Charlotte was the only one who paid more than a fleeting visit to London, and Yorkshire must rightfully claim them, but their publishers, Smith Elder and Co., were in London at 65 Cornhill, in the City. Anne and Charlotte paid their first visit to Mr Smith in 1848. The present building on the site (now No. 32) has a carved door and one of the door panels shows them meeting Thackeray there. They are also commemorated by a tablet, presented by the Brontë Society, in Poets' Corner, Westminster Abbey.

ELIZABETH BROUGHTON

1590?–1640?
Fleet Street, EC4

Of a respectable family, Elizabeth was probably born at the old manor house at Canon Pyon, Herefordshire. When her father discovered that she had been seduced by a penniless young man, he locked her up in a turret, but she climbed down by a rope and ran off to London. Once there, she 'set herself up' and, being very beautiful, was also very expensive. Although she was the mistress of the Earl of Dorset for a while, her speciality seems to have been quantity rather than quality and John Aubrey in his *Brief Lives* remembered an old song about her (sung as a litany):

> From the watch at twelve o'clock,
> And from Bess Broughton's
> buttoned smock
> Libera nos Domine.

In fact, it is John Aubrey who gave her her only known epitaph: 'At last she grew common and infamous and gott the pox, of which she died.'

ELIZABETH BARRETT BROWNING

1806–1861
(née Barrett)
Married: St Marylebone Church, Marylebone Road, NW1;
Plaque: 50 Wimpole Street, W1

> Earth's crammed with Heaven,
> And every common bush afire with
> God.   (from *Aurora Leigh*)

Never particularly robust, by the time she was twenty-nine and the family had moved to London, Elizabeth Barrett seemed to have become a confirmed invalid. A volume of her poetry was published and then, on the recommendation of her doctor, she went to stay in Torquay. While she was there, a favourite brother was drowned in a boating accident and her health deteriorated rapidly. On her return to Wimpole Street she was advised to stay in her room, avoid exercise and receive very few visitors, a régime of which her father strongly approved. Elizabeth occupied her time by writing poetry and writing to friends.

An admirer of Robert Browning's work, she included his name in one of her poems. Flattered, he wrote to her and she replied. When he suggested a meeting she finally agreed and Robert began an enthusiastic courtship which was concealed from Elizabeth's father. Her health improved. She began to go out and, in 1846, they were secretly married in St Marylebone Parish Church. A week later they left the country for France; Elizabeth's father never forgave her.

The Brownings settled in Italy where Elizabeth gave birth to a son, enjoyed a normal social life and continued to write poetry; her *Aurora Leigh* was published in 1856. She died in Florence and was buried there, in the Protestant cemetery.

FRANCES HODGSON BURNETT

**1849–1924
(née Hodgson)**
Plaque: 63 Portland Place,
WI

The acceptance of the belief that
this is only a world of sorrows is
hideous and ought to be
exterminated.

Frances Hodgson was born in
Manchester and emigrated to
America with her family when she
was almost sixteen. They settled in
Tennessee and Frances began to
write. In 1868 her first published
story 'Hearts and Diamonds'
appeared in the popular women's
magazine, *Godey's Lady's Book*.
She married Dr Swan Burnett in
1873 and the following year gave
birth to a son, Lionel. Her first
novel, *That Lass O' Lowrie's* was
serialised in *Scribner's Magazine* in
1876, the year that her second son,
Vivian, was born.

Vivian was to be the model for
Frances Hodgson Burnett's
best-known hero, *Little Lord
Fauntleroy* (1886), a bestseller that
made her wealthy and famous in
both America and England. She
settled in England after the death
of her elder son, renting 63
Portland Place in London where
she wrote *A Lady of Quality*
(1896). Two years later she
divorced her husband and rented
Maytham Hall, in Kent, as a
country home. She wrote

continuously, and many of her
novels were dramatised. A second
marriage – to Stephen Townsend,
an English surgeon with ambitions
as an actor – proved to be a
short-lived disaster and Frances
eventually returned to America.
She died at her home in Plandome,
Long Island and was buried not far
away at God's Acre, Roslyn.

Little Lord Fauntleroy may still
be Frances Hodgson Burnett's
most famous work, but it is her
book *The Secret Garden* (1911)
with its heroine, the
'disagreeable-looking' little girl,
Mary Lennox, that remains one of
the most enchanting stories about
childhood ever written. It was
serialised on television in 1975:

> She took another long breath . . .
> held back the swinging curtain of
> ivy and pushed back the door which
> opened slowly – slowly.
> Then she slipped through it, and
> shut it behind her, and stood with
> her back against it, looking about
> her and breathing quite fast with
> excitement, and wonder, and
> delight.
> She was standing *inside* the secret
> garden.

FANNY (FRANCES) BURNEY

1752–1840
(**Madame D'Arblay**)
Plaque: 11 Bolton Street,
W1

'Little Fanny Burney', as Dr Johnson liked to call her, had her first novel, *Evelina*, published anonymously in 1778. It was a great success and when her authorship was discovered, she became a celebrity. Her novel *Cecilia* soon followed. In 1786 she accepted the post of Second Keeper of the Robes to Queen Charlotte. Fanny lived at Windsor Castle and at Kew and was thoroughly miserable.

Finally able to resign through ill health, she married Monsieur D'Arblay, an almost penniless French exile, and, in 1794, gave birth to a son. The D'Arblays lived in France for ten years, and then returned to England. Fanny continued to write, but her next book *The Wanderer* (1814) was given a hostile reception, Lord Macaulay hoping that: '. . . no judicious friend to the Author's memory will attempt to draw it from the oblivion into which it has justly fallen.'

After her husband's death she moved to 11 Bolton Street, near Piccadilly (where there is now a plaque) and began to prepare the memoirs of her father, Dr Burney. She was buried at Walcot, near Bath.

ISABEL BURTON

1831–1896
(**née Arundell**)
Buried: with Richard Burton, Mortlake Cemetery, Mortlake

Tomb of Richard and Isabel at St Mary Magdalen's Churchyard, Mortlake.
'I am waiting for a welcome sound – the tinkling of his camel bell'

Isabel was a strong-willed woman and a devout Catholic who worshipped her husband, Richard Burton. He was an explorer, an Arabic scholar, a rebel and probably an agnostic. They were married for thirty years.

Isabel rode and fenced with him. When he felt like it, she accompanied him on his travels; when he felt like it, she was sent home. She acted as his secretary and, encouraged by him, she wrote herself.

It is said that, as he lay dying in Trieste, she persuaded the doctor to apply electrodes to his heart – to keep him alive until a priest could administer the last rites. After his death she burnt, among other things, the manuscript of his translation of Arabian erotica, *The Scented Garden*. Richard Burton's body was buried in the Catholic cemetery at Mortlake in a stone replica of an Arab tent; the door, when opened, set camel-bells ringing. Living in a house near Baker Street and also in her cottage near the cemetery, Isabel began to write his biography. When she had finished it, she destroyed his private diaries. Then there was nothing left for her to do.

> Reader! I have paid, I have packed and I have suffered. I am waiting to join his caravan. I am waiting for a welcome sound – the tinkling of his camel-bell.

FRANCES MARY BUSS

1827–1894
Buried: Theydon Bois
Church Graveyard, near
Epping, (Memorial
window inside the
church)

As I have grown older, the terrible sufferings of women of my own class, for want of good elementary training, have more than ever intensified my earnest desire to lighten . . . the misery of women brought up 'to be married and taken care of', and left alone in the world destitute.

Miss Buss founded the North London Collegiate School for girls (now at Canons, in Edgware). She was Head Mistress for over forty years and when, in 1870, it was handed over to a body of trustees, it became the first public day school for girls. Although they barely knew each other, her name has been inextricably linked with that of Dorothea Beale (q.v.), in a teasing schoolgirls' rhyme:

> Miss Buss and Miss Beale
> Cupid's darts do not feel.
> How different from us,
> Miss Beale and Miss Buss.

LADY ELIZABETH BUTLER

1846–1933
(née Thompson)
Royal Academy of Art,
Piccadilly, W1

An artist who concentrated on military themes, Lady Butler's first major success was a painting named *The Roll Call*. Painted in her studio in the Fulham Road, it was shown at the Royal Academy Exhibition in 1874; a policeman had to be posted by it to control the crowds. Her fame was instantaneous, so much so that a quarter of a million copies of her photograph sold within weeks. In her autobiography she wrote:

> Indeed, one of my aunts, passing along the street in Chelsea, was astonished to see her rueful niece on a costermonger's barrow amongst some bananas!

Born near Lausanne in Switzerland, she married Major (later Lieutenant-General) Butler in 1877, travelled extensively and died in Ireland. Her painting *Scotland for Ever* (Leeds City Art Gallery) was exhibited in 1978 at the Royal Academy exhibition, 'Great Victorian Painters'. An incredibly dramatic cavalry charge, galloping straight out of the canvas, many people now consider this to be her masterpiece.

JOSEPHINE BUTLER

1828–1906
(née Grey)
Stained-glass window: St
Olave's Church, Hart
Street, EC3

There is no evil in the world so great that God cannot raise up to meet it a corresponding beauty and glory which will blaze it out of countenance.

Josephine Butler was one of the most passionate and single-minded reformers of the nineteenth century. Married to George Butler in 1852, she suffered a terrible personal tragedy when their six-year-old daughter fell from the banisters at their home and died of her injuries.

A fierce campaigner against the exploitation of women, she founded a home for 'fallen women' in Winchester and became involved when the journalist W. T.

Stead decided to expose the scandal of child prostitution [see Rebecca Jarrett]. Her major battle, however, was waged against the Contagious Diseases Act of 1864.

This act provided for the compulsory medical examination in certain areas – mainly sea-ports and garrison towns – of women suspected of being prostitutes. Furiously indignant over the injustice of women being humiliated and punished when men got off scot-free, Josephine sprang into action. She used every weapon at her disposal, and a petition launched her brilliant campaign. Organising Ladies' Associations all over the country as

Stained glass window in
St Olave's Church, Hart
Street, EC3 depicts
Josephine Butler,
Elizabeth Fry, Edith
Cavell, Florence
Nightingale and
Elizabeth I

a back-up force, she spoke at meetings, wrote manifestos and pamphlets, argued and prayed. She visited licensed brothels, travelled abroad to study conditions there, wrote reports and prayed even harder. Finally, victory was hers. In 1886 the Repeal Bill was introduced and gained the Royal Assent.

Josephine Butler loved music, climbing mountains and sketching out of doors. Among her many published works, she wrote a life of Catherine of Siena and a study called *Women's Work and Women's Culture*. Born at Milfield, in Northumberland, she died at Wooler in the same county.

DAME CLARA BUTT

1873–1936
The Royal Albert Hall, Kensington Gore, SW7; Plaque: 7 Harley Road, NW3

Clara Butt was a tall woman with an exceptionally powerful voice, described as having a trombone-like boom in its lower register. Someone once remarked that the Albert Hall must have been built in intelligent anticipation of her advent. She won a scholarship to the Royal College of Music in London and made her debut as Ursula in Sullivan's *Golden Legend*. After singing the title-role in *Orpheus* at the Lyceum her success was assured.

Clara married the baritone Kennerly Rumford and had two children. Elgar wrote *Sea Pictures* for her, and his *Land of Hope and Glory* virtually became her signature tune. Born in Sussex, she died at North Stoke, Oxfordshire.

MARIA, LADY CALLCOTT

1785–1842
(née Dundas)
Buried: Kensal Green Cemetery, NW10

A great part of her early life was spent either at sea or in travel, and to the last no subject was more animating to her than a ship, and no hero excited her enthusiasm to so high a degree as Nelson. (*The Gentleman's Magazine*, January 1843)

Maria was the daughter of Rear-Admiral Dundas and in 1809

married Captain Thomas Graham, R.N. She travelled extensively throughout India, returning to England in 1811, where she published an account of her travels and then moved to Italy. There she wrote *The Memoirs of the Life of Poussin* (1820). She was in South America in 1822, the year her husband died at sea, and remaining there for a while, became governess to the daughter of Don Pedro, Emperor of Brazil.

In 1826 Maria married the landscape painter Augustus Callcott. Four years later she was seriously ill and became a permanent invalid, confined to her room, at their house in Kensington, where she wrote her best-seller, *Little Arthur's History of England* (1835). When the Century Edition was published in 1936, it was reviewed with enthusiasm in the *Cornhill Magazine*:

> It has lain on thousands of schoolroom tables, been thumbed by thousands of hot, childish hands; been 'mugged up', delighted in, probably wept over. Its hundred-years-old face is as fresh and engaging as ever.

JULIA CAMERON

1815–1879
(née Pattle)
Lived: Carslake Road,
Putney Heath, SW15
(house demolished)

... These productions by Miss Cameron ... are among the few figure subjects here which have any decided art value in their lighting.
Illustrated London News, 1865

... In these pictures all that is good in photography has been neglected ...
Photographic Journal, 1865

Julia Cameron should be an inspiration to women who feel that life grinds to a depressing halt after the age of forty. She plunged enthusiastically into photography when she was forty-eight, and, controversial as her achievements were in her lifetime, in 1974 her portrait of Mrs Duckworth was sold at Sotheby's for £1,500.

Born in Calcutta, buried in Ceylon, she lived for many years in England (her homes in London were at East Sheen and Putney Heath). A brilliant amateur, dedicated to the point of dottiness, she recorded many of the beautiful, famous and talented people of her day. Her relations often remembered her with amused awe:

> ... Aunt Julia appeared as a terrifying elderly woman, short and squat, with none of the Pattle grace and beauty about her. Dressed in dark clothes, stained with chemicals from her photography (and smelling of them too), with a plump eager face and piercing eyes, and a voice husky and a little harsh, yet in some way compelling and even charming. (Laura Troubridge, *Memoirs and Reflections*)

MRS PATRICK CAMPBELL

1865–1940
(née Tanner)
Plaque: 33 Kensington
Square, W8

Mrs Campbell, born in Kensington, took up acting at the age of twenty-three. The role that made her famous was Paula Tanqueray in Pinero's *The Second Mrs Tanqueray*, which opened at the St James's Theatre in 1893.

Her first husband, Patrick Campbell, was killed in the South African war and, in 1914, she married George Cornwallis-West. In the same year she played Eliza Doolittle in *Pygmalion*, a part written especially for her by her close friend, George Bernard Shaw.

After 1929 she left England and travelled to Hollywood, New York and then Paris. Her excuse for refusing to return was that her beloved dog, Moonbeam, would have had to go into quarantine. She died at Pau, in France, and was buried there.

Mrs Patrick Campbell was a unique and brilliant, if sometimes difficult and temperamental, actress. After her death Sir John Gielgud, who had known and worked with her, wrote:

> In some lectures which she gave in London not many years ago, when she held the stage alone for over an hour, speaking wisely and wittily about acting, and giving many wonderful excerpts from her famous parts, she showed to many of us who loved her a beauty and mystery which I for one shall never forget. 'There's a great spirit gone.'
> *The Times*, 1940

BETTY CARELESS

d. 1752
St Paul's Church, Covent
Garden, WC2

A close scrutiny of the eighth picture in Hogarth's *A Rake's Progress* series ('A Scene in a Mad House') reveals an inmate crazed with love; he has carved the name of the cause of his despair on a stair-railing nearby – 'Charming Betty Careless'.

Although unrecorded, her exploits must have been as devastating as Hogarth's comment implies. When she died the *Gentleman's Magazine* published this obituary:

Was buried from the poor house of St Paul's Covent Garden, the famed Betty Careless: who had helped the gay gentlemen of this nation to squander above 50,000L [pounds].

JANE WELSH CARLYLE

**1801–1866
(née Baillie Welsh)**
Lived: 24 Cheyne Row,
Chelsea, SW3

If you wish for a quiet life, never you marry a dyspeptic man of genius.

The Carlyles married in Scotland in 1826 and, eight years later, moved into their new home, 5 (now 24) Cheyne Row, Chelsea. Their marriage was not a tranquil one. Thomas Carlyle, historian, philosopher and author, suffered from bilious attacks and could only work, he said, in *total* silence. Jane, desperately trying to organise their life around his needs – including the supervision of a 'sound-proof' attic for his study – often suffered from headaches, insomnia and nervous tension.

Jane Carlyle's home at 24
Cheyne Row, Chelsea

Her letters, published by James Froude in 1883, are delightfully lively and crackle with a dry, caustic, sense of humour:

Such a noise about that 'Royal Marriage'! I wish it were over. People are so woefully like sheep – all running where they see others run . . . Have you heard of that wonderful Bishop Colenso? Such a talk about him too. And he isn't worth talking about for five minutes, except for the absurdity of a man making arithmetical onslaughts on the Pentateuch, with a *Bishop's little black silk apron on!*

Jane had a fine, analytical mind and her observations are both vivid and revealing, as when she described the Count d'Orsay's visit to Cheyne Row:

Carlyle in his grey plaid suit, and his tub chair, looking blandly at the Prince of Dandies; and the Prince of Dandies . . . all resplendent as a diamond-beetle, looking blandly at *him*. D'Orsay is a really handsome man, after one has heard him speak and found that he has both wit and sense; but at first sight his beauty is of that rather disgusting sort which seems to be like genius, 'of no sex'.

In spite of their difficulties, the Carlyles' devotion for each other was very deep. After her death, Thomas, heartbroken, wrote the inscription for Jane's grave in Haddington, Scotland, which ends with the words:

She died at London, 21st April 1866; suddenly snatched away from him, and the light of his life as if gone out.

MARGARET CARPENTER

1793–1872
(née Geddes)
Exhibited: Royal Academy of Art, Piccadilly, W1

Born in Salisbury, Wiltshire, Margaret Geddes was given lessons in painting and figure drawing by a local teacher and later allowed to 'copy' in Lord Radnor's gallery at Longford Castle. He encouraged her to send work to the Society of Arts and, in 1814, she moved to London and exhibited at the Academy, thus beginning her successful career as a portrait painter.

In 1817 Margaret married W. H. Carpenter, who later became Keeper of Prints and

Drawings at the British Museum; they had several children. She died in London and was soon forgotten, although the *Art Journal* of 1873 made a gallant protest on her behalf:

Had the Royal Academy abrogated the law which denies a female admission to its ranks, Mrs Carpenter would most assuredly have gained, as she merited, a place in them; but we despair of ever living to see the rights of women vindicated in this respect.

DORA CARRINGTON

1893–1932
Trained: Slade School of Fine Art, Gower Street, WC1
See Gwen John

Trained at the Slade School of Fine Art, Dora Carrington showed a marked ability as a painter. Her relationships with people, both men and women, were always complicated and often ambiguous. This may have hampered the progress of her work, although her landscapes have a delightfully 'naïve' style and her portraits are often bold in conception and execution. She designed the wood-cut decorations for Leonard and Virginia Woolf's first Hogarth Press publication, *Two Stories* by Virginia and L. S. Woolf (1917).

She had affairs with Mark Gertler, the painter, Gerald Brenan, the writer, and married

Ralph Partridge; but the most important relationship of her life was with Lytton Strachey, writer, intellectual and homosexual. David Garnett in his preface to *Carrington – Letters and Extracts from her Diaries* (1970) wrote:

They became lovers, but physical love was made difficult and became impossible. The trouble on Lytton's side was his diffidence and feeling of inadequacy, and his being perpetually attracted by young men; and on Carrington's side her intense dislike of being a woman which gave her a feeling of inferiority so that a normal and joyful relationship was next to impossible.

Nevertheless, their life together at the Old Mill in Tidmarsh and at Ham Spray in Wiltshire, was often very happy. Joined by Ralph Partridge, Carrington's husband, they entertained large numbers of guests at both of the homes that she had helped to create.

After Strachey's death Dora Carrington committed suicide at Ham Spray House. She had asked that her ashes should be buried under some laurels in the garden there and her wishes were carried out.

ELIZABETH CARTER
1717–1806
Buried: Grosvenor Chapel, South Audley Street, W1 (unmarked)

'My old friend, Mrs Carter,' said Dr Johnson, 'could make a pudding as well as translate Epictetus from the Greek and work a handkerchief as well as compose a poem.'

The translation, *All the Works of Epictetus now Extant*, was published in 1758 – but that was not all Elizabeth could do. She studied astronomy and ancient history, learnt Latin, French, Hebrew, Italian and Spanish, played both the spinet and the flute, walked ten miles at a stretch and still found time to form romantic relationships with other women.

The (understandable) problem of not being able to wake up early enough she solved easily. Boswell described how:

At a certain hour, her chamber-light should burn a string to which a heavy weight was suspended, which then fell with a strong, sudden noise: this roused her from her sleep . . . and she had no difficulty in getting up.

Born in Deal, Kent, she visited London regularly, often attending Elizabeth Montagu's intellectual salon.

EDITH CAVELL
1865–1915
Statue: St Martin's Place, WC2

In 1895 Edith Cavell applied to the Fountains Fever Hospital in Tooting, London, to become an Assistant Nurse, Class II, and was accepted. She had previously worked as a governess, the last four years having been spent in Belgium, teaching the children of a Brussels lawyer. After Tooting, she moved to the London Hospital, where she trained and worked for over four years. 'E. Cavell was steady and nice minded.' (Final report by Miss Lückes, Matron)

In 1907, following a period of restlessness, she was invited to become the matron of one of Belgium's first training-schools for nurses and accepted the post with alacrity. By 1912 she had helped to establish a first-rate teaching-hospital with a staff of fifty nurses. Her holidays were almost always spent in England and, on 3 August, 1914, she returned to Brussels after one of those visits. The following day, England declared war on Germany, the Germans invaded Belgium and in September Edith wrote to her sister:

All is quiet just now and life goes on in many ways as usual. At present we have few patients but are affiliated to the Red Cross and may later under different conditions have much work to do.

Two months later the first 'visitors' arrived – one Belgian and two British soldiers – led there by a complicated escape route. Edith Cavell received them, as she continued to receive the steady trickle of soldiers who reached the hospital at weekly intervals. She was one of the final links in the route and was, naturally, in danger.

In June, 1915, German officers raided the hospital but left empty-handed. In August they returned and this time arrested Nurse Elizabeth Wilkins and Edith Cavell. Elizabeth Wilkins was later released, but Edith spent ten weeks in prison before the trial, which took place between 7 and 11 October. Five of those arrested were condemned to death, including Edith.

News of the execution reached England on 16 October and a

On the statue:

HUMANITY

EDITH CAVELL
BRUSSELS
DAWN
OCTOBER 12TH
1915
PATRIOTISM IS NOT ENOUGH
I MUST HAVE NO HATRED OR
BITTERNESS FOR ANYONE

tremendous wave of emotion surged through the country. After the war her body was exhumed and brought back to be buried in Norfolk where she had been born.

In 1920 her statue, by George Frampton, was unveiled in St Martin's Place, just north of Trafalgar Square. The inscription includes her own words:

> Patriotism is not enough. I must have no hatred or bitterness for anyone.

Left, memorial to Edith Cavell in St Martin's Place, WC2 and right, her dog Jack, stuffed, in the Imperial War Museum

HESTER CHAPONE

**1727–1801
(née Mulso)**
St James's Place, SW1

In consequence of his questioning her strictly on what she believed to be the Duties of the Married State, Hester Mulso once wrote a 'Matrimonial Creed' for her friend, Samuel Richardson, the novelist. She included this statement:

> Notwithstanding this acknowledged superiority of right of command, I believe it highly conducive, and, to delicate minds, absolutely necessary to conjugal happiness that the husband have such an opinion of his wife's understanding, principles, and integrity of heart, as would induce him to exalt her to the rank of his first and dearest friend, and to endow her, by his own free gift, with all the privileges, rights, and freedoms of the most perfect friendship.

In 1760 she married Mr Chapone, in London but, widowed in less than a year, was denied the opportunity of testing her own theories.

Born in Northamptonshire, she wrote *The Loves of Amoret and Melissa* at the age of nine. Her most admired work was her *Letters on the Improvement of the Mind* (1774), originally letters written to a niece and then published as a book. Hester Chapone knew Dr Johnson, kept up a lively correspondence with Elizabeth Carter (q.v.) and was a close friend of Mary Delany (q.v.).

DAME AGATHA CHRISTIE

**1890–1976
(née Miller)**
St Martin's Theatre, West Street, WC2

Born in Torquay, Agatha married Archibald Christie in 1914. Her first detective story, *The Mysterious Affair at Styles* was published in 1920 and introduced, for the first time, her famous detective-hero Hercule Poirot. When she died, her play *The Mousetrap* was in its twenty-fourth year at the St Martin's Theatre in London. She is said to be the most widely read British author in the world.

Agatha Christie divorced her first husband in 1928 after a mysterious episode when she disappeared for ten days and was discovered in a hotel in Harrogate, apparently suffering from amnesia. In 1930 she married the archaeologist, Max Mallowan. She became an exceptionally wealthy woman, was made DBE in 1971 and died at her home in Wallingford, Oxfordshire.

SUSANNAH CIBBER

1714–1766
(née Arne)
Buried: North Walk,
Westminster Abbey
Cloisters

The first performance of Handel's *Messiah* took place in Dublin in 1742. Tutored by Handel himself, who had long admired the tragic quality of her unique voice, Susannah Cibber sang 'He shall feed his flock' and 'He was despised and rejected of men'.

Born in King Street, Covent Garden, Susannah came from a musical family (her brother, Thomas, composed, among other delights, 'Rule Britannia'), but she also revealed considerable talent as an actress. Her father persuaded her into a disastrous marriage with the notorious actor-manager, Theophilus Cibber, who treated her badly, appropriated most of her earnings and then pushed her into the arms of one of her admirers, William Sloper. When the liaison proved unprofitable Theophilus (loudly and publicly accusing her of infidelity and desertion) demanded her return. Susannah survived the scandal, living quietly in the country with Mr Sloper and, after her success in *Messiah*, appeared again on the London stage.

GWEN CLARKE

1910–1978
(née Williams)
Franciscan Road,
Tooting, SW17

A descendant of the Welsh hymn-writer, William Williams, of Pantycelin, Gwen Williams took her BA at Swansea University, and in 1931 married Waldo Clarke. They lived for some years in Egypt, where they both taught, and where their first daughter was born, but returned to England before the Second World War. After the birth of a second daughter, they moved to London and Gwen began to teach again. Convinced that the most important stage in a child's learning comes at the very beginning, she moved from Secondary School teaching to the challenge of Infant School education, and eventually became Headmistress of Franciscan Road Infants' School in Tooting. She specialised in the teaching of 'number' to small children and lectured on the methods of Catherine Sterne.

Gwen Clarke retired with her husband to Wales and died in Southgate on the Gower coast, leaving four grandchildren. Her two daughters wrote this book.

MARY ANNE CLARKE

1778–1852?
(née Thompson)
Lived: Gloucester Place,
W1

The British public, always fascinated by royal scandals, were delighted when Frederick, Duke of York, second son of George III and Commander-in-Chief of the British Army, was publicly made a fool of by his ex-mistress, Mary Anne Clarke. During an enquiry, in 1809, into his conduct, '. . . with regard to promotions, exchanges and appointments to commissions . . .' Mary Clarke enjoyed herself too. Intelligent, witty and vengeful, she assured the House of Commons that she *had* regularly taken money offered to her to influence the Duke over army promotions. His love-letters were read out in public and, at the end of the proceedings, although he was not found guilty of corruption, the humiliated Duke resigned as Commander-in-Chief and also gave up his current mistress, a Mrs Carey:

O pity, pity me,
In future I'll be wary,
I never, never will
Kiss either Clarke or Carey.

Years earlier Mary had met the Duke, captivated him and moved into Gloucester Place. Wildly extravagant, she had been served with a summons for debt in 1806 and the Duke, fearful of scandal, ended the affair, giving her the lease of the house and promising an annuity. When no allowance appeared, Mary threatened to publish his letters. Ignored, her chance came when, having boasted of her recent influence over the Duke to a Member of Parliament, the enquiry was called.

Mary Clarke's downfall was due

to her greed. Not satisfied by her triumphant revenge, she threatened to publish her memoirs and was paid off with ten thousand pounds; after that was spent, her next attempt to publish landed her in court for libel. After nine uneventful months in prison she left to live in France and sank into oblivion.

KITTY (CATHERINE) CLIVE

1711–1785 (née Raftor)
Memorial Plaque: St Mary's Church, Twickenham

Clive, sir, is a good thing to sit by; she always understands what you say . . . (Dr Samuel Johnson)

I love to sit by Dr Johnson; he always entertains me . . . (Kitty Clive)

Kitty Clive, born in London, became a great comic actress and a rival of Peg Woffington. Her marriage to George Clive did not last long and ended in separation by mutual consent. She worked at Drury Lane and then joined David Garrick's company until her retirement in 1769.

Horace Walpole, who was very fond of her, gave her a cottage in the grounds of his home, Strawberry Hill, Twickenham. When she died he placed an urn in the shrubbery there and composed the inscription:

Ye smiles and jests, still hover round;
This is mirth's consecrated ground.
Here lived the laughter-loving dame,
A matchless actress, Clive her name;
The comic muse with her retired,
And shed a tear when she expired.

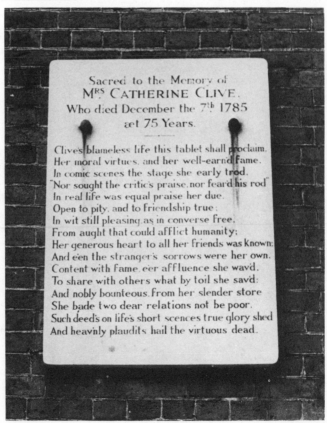

ELEANOR COADE

d. 1796

ELEANOR COADE

d. 1821

Example of 'Coadestone': Captain Bligh's tomb, St Mary-at-Lambeth, SE1

Coadestone figures outside Church of St Andrew, Holborn

All over London there are statues and memorials made of 'Coadestone'. The material was named after two energetic Eleanors, mother and daughter, who originally ran a pottery business in Lyme Regis. It was here that they met a young man, Richard Holt, who had taken out a patent for a method of making a substance that had the appearance of stone. He had opened a factory in Lambeth, but became ill and went bankrupt. The Coades bought his factory and stock and moved to London in 1769.

The following year Mr Coade died. Undaunted, the two Eleanors carried on the business, which went from strength to strength. Part of their success was due to the employment of high quality artists, part to their undoubted talent for brilliant salesmanship. After her mother's death, Eleanor Coade Junior was joined by her cousin, John Sealy, and in 1799 they organised an exhibition at the factory. It was after visiting this exhibition that Captain Bligh (of the *Bounty*) ordered his Coadestone tomb, which can be seen at the church of St Mary-at-Lambeth.

Mother and daughter were both buried in Bunhill Fields, the Non-Conformist cemetery, but the tomb was destroyed during the Second World War.

ELIZABETH COBBOLD

1767–1824
(née Knipe)
Born: Watling Street, EC4
(exact site unknown)

Elizabeth Knipe, of Watling Street in the City of London, wrote poetry from an early age and, in 1787, her *Six Narrative Poems* was published, confidently dedicated to Sir Joshua Reynolds. Two years later she married a Mr William Clarke and embarked on a two-volume romance called *The Sword, or Father Bertrand's History of His Own Times*. Left a widow at the tender age of twenty-three, she then met and married John Cobbold, a wealthy widower of Ipswich, who already had fourteen children. Elizabeth added seven more to his collection, continued to write, and somehow also found time for charitable work. (She helped to found a society for 'Clothing the Infant Poor'.)

Under the pseudonym of 'Carolina Petty Pasty', her poetical skit *The Mince Pye* was published in 1800. Her sense of humour had surfaced several times before, perhaps the most endearing example being in this wry self-portrait:

> In neatness no excelling pattern,
> Nor yet affectedly a slattern.
> Too proud to cringe, too plain to shine,
> She quits all claim at twenty-nine
> To dissipation or to fame,
> A fat, unfashionable, dame.

LOTTIE COLLINS

1866–1910
Plaque commemorating the Gaiety Theatre on the Citibank, east end of Strand, WC2

> A smart and stylish girl you see,
> The Belle of High Society,
> Fond of fun as fond can be –
> When it's on the strict Q.T.
> Not too young and not too old,
> Not too timid, not too bold,
> But just the very thing, I'm told,
> That in your arms you'd like to hold . . .
> Ta – ra – ra – BOOM – de – ay.

Lottie's song. A smash hit in 1891 . . . and even now people nod . . . yes, yet of course . . . 'Ta – ra – ra – boom – de – ay'. Only the echo . . . but how stunning it must have been. Lottie Collins, in a large hat, red dress . . . standing, demure and restrained, to sing each verse and then, suddenly, the chorus . . .

'Ta – ra –' Lottie, a high-kicking whirlwind of swirling petticoats, the band full blast, the audience roaring it out with her – 'ra – BOOM – de–ay!'

She sang it at the Grand Theatre in Islington . . . she sang it at the Gaiety . . . two hundred pounds a week . . . and then she waved goodbye for a while . . . she was off to America. The children took over:

> Lottie Collins has no drawers,
> Will you kindly lend her yours?
> She is going far away
> To sing Ta – ra – ra – boom – de – ay!

EMMA CONS

1837–1912
Old Vic Theatre, SE1;
Plaque: 136 Seymour Place, W1

In a sense it is strange that the name of Emma Cons should be remembered in connection with the Old Vic, which she called her recreation. (Lilian Baylis)

Born in London, Emma Cons studied at the School of Ornamental Art for Females in Gower Street. Later she became the first woman to be employed by Powell's Whitefriars factory as a designer and restorer of stained-glass windows. Through her friend, Octavia Hill (q.v.), she became involved in housing reform and helped to collect rents for Miss Hill's slum property improvement scheme.

In 1879 Emma launched out on her own, and having bought Surrey Lodge in Lambeth, formed the South London Dwelling Company. Then, hoping to provide an alternative to heavy drinking in public houses, she leased the Victoria Theatre near Waterloo Station, and opened it as the Royal Victoria Coffee and Music Hall in 1880. This was the birth of the 'Old Vic' as it later became known.

Emma Cons also became an alderman of the newly-created London County Council in 1889, although she resigned when two women councillors were challenged and unseated. She died in Hever, Kent, and her ashes were scattered in a wood near by. Her niece, Lilian Baylis (q.v.), took over the Old Vic after her death.

MARIE CORELLI

1855–1924
(**Mary Mackay**)
Plaque: 47 Longridge Road, Kensington, SW5

Mocked by the critics, read avidly by an insatiable public, Marie Corelli was one of Queen Victoria's favourite authors. She wrote highly colourful moral romances and became one of the first British 'best-sellers'. Her *Barabbas* attracted a deluge of adverse criticism, but sold ten thousand copies in the first week of publication.

Although she lived in London for much of her life, in 1901 she settled permanently in Mason's Croft, Stratford-upon-Avon, with her lifelong friend (and biographer) Bertha Vyver. She derived much enjoyment from appearing regularly on the River Avon in a gondola, shipped especially from Venice. The inhabitants of Stratford soon became used to her antics and were quite sorry when she died. She was buried in the cemetery there, on the Evesham Road.

Marie Corelli's house at 47 Longridge Road, SW5

ANGELA BURDETT-COUTTS

1814–1906

Buried: Westminster
Abbey, SW1;
Statue: entrance to Holly
Village, Swains Lane, N6

Statue on gateway to
Holly Village, Swain's
Lane, Highgate, the
model village created by
Angela Burdett-Coutts

At the age of twenty-three, Angela became one of the richest women in Europe. She was a granddaughter of Thomas Coutts, the banker, and this fortune was left to her by his second wife [see Harriot Mellon].

Shy – and isolated by her wealth – she proceeded to channel large sums into 'good causes'. With Charles Dickens, she founded a home for 'fallen women' (and paid for the education of his son Charley). She gave support, and practical aid, to Florence Nightingale (q.v.) and Dr Livingstone, and helped destitute children in Stepney. She paid for one hundred emigrants to be sent from Ireland to Canada during the Irish famine, created the model 'Holly Village' at the bottom of

47

Swain's Lane, Highgate, founded Bishoprics in Cape Town and Adelaide and paid for St Stephen's church, and school, in Rochester Row, Westminster. Queen Victoria bestowed a peerage on her in 1871.

Angela Burdett-Coutts once proposed marriage to the Duke of Wellington when he was seventy-eight and she was thirty-three. He gently, but firmly, declined and they remained good friends. When *she* was in her seventies, she horrified society by marrying William Ashmead Bartlett, who was half her age. It was not an unqualified success.

ANN CURTIS

1764–1838
(later Hatton)
(née Kemble)
Schomberg House, Pall Mall, SW1 (site of the 'Temple of Health')

Positively the Last Night Mrs SIDDONS'S youngest sister, Mrs CURTIS desires most respectfully to inform the Public that THIS EVENING she will read a Lecture at the TEMPLE of HEALTH in PALL-MALL, on the present state and influence of WOMEN on Society . . . etc.

When the dignified and respectable actress Sarah Siddons (q.v.) saw the above, she must have wished that her 'youngest sister' had never been born. Not only was the 'Temple of Health' run by a notorious quack, Dr Graham, but lectures given there were of a dubious nature. This was clearly another move in the war of nerves that Ann Curtis was waging against her famous sister.

When she was a girl, Ann, prevented by lameness from following the rest of the Kembles on to the stage, had taken to writing. In 1783 a volume of her poetry was published and the same year she married a Mr Curtis and moved to London. Almost immediately, a notice appeared in the papers pleading for '. . . Donations in favour of Mrs Curtis, youngest sister of Mrs Siddons'. She was, it seemed, in distressed circumstances and her family had 'flatly refused her'. A little later came the embarrassing 'Lectures' in Pall-Mall and other minor irritations; then, more dramatically, a rumour that Mrs Curtis had attempted to poison herself in Westminster Abbey (but had recovered) . . . and then a lull.

The uneasy peace was shattered by an incident reported in the *Morning Herald*. Ann had somehow got into conversation one evening with a gentleman from Staines, carrying – or so he thought – an unloaded pistol. Teasingly, he had pointed the weapon at himself a couple of times and pulled the trigger . . . nothing happened. When he levelled it at Ann, however, it had gone off in her face. 'Mr Cruikshank, who attends her,' the paper solemnly related, 'has no hopes of her recovery'. She recovered again.

This time the family had had enough. Ann was offered an annuity on condition that she lived at least 150 miles from London. She married a second time and finally settled, rather reluctantly, in Swansea. Ann published several books of verse and fiction, became known as 'Ann of Swansea' and died in Park Street there.

> In vain by various griefs opprest,
> I vagrant roam devoid of rest.
> With aching heart, still lingring
>   stray
> Around the shores of Swansea Bay.

ANNE SEYMOUR DAMER

1749–1828
(née Conway)
Statue: British Museum,
Great Russell Street, WC1

At the far end of the King's Library in the British Museum, at the bottom of a staircase, stands an attractive statue of a woman. At her feet, just showing beneath the folds of her dress, are some sculptor's tools and one arm cradles a strange little figure of what appears to be a river-god. It is the work of Giuseppe Ceracchi, and the inscription reads simply: 'The Hon. Mrs Anne Seymour Damer, 1749–1828'.

The daughter of Field-Marshal Conway, Anne married John

Damer in 1767. A 'black sheep' and a spendthrift he shot himself in dubious company, at a tavern near Covent Garden. Anne, already a gifted amateur, took up sculpture seriously. She had lessons from Giuseppe Ceracchi, worked in John Bacon's studio, studied anatomy under Cruikshank, and had some of her work exhibited at the Royal Academy.

> . . . Mrs Damer put up a shed in the garden at Strawberry Hill, and there did I watch with great curiosity the progress of that very good-natured woman, but bad sculptor, in spoiling marble. (Maria Callcott)

> . . . She modelled her designs herself, and also, it is admitted, worked on the marble with her own hands; but the finish of her work in this material shows that she must have been assisted by a skilled artist. (*Redgrave's Dictionary of Artists of the English School*)

It is difficult to find evidence to justify either of these statements. Anne's bust of Sir Joseph Banks (British Museum) looks both attractive and professional (her self-portrait, also owned by the British Museum, was destroyed during the last war) and the 'heads' of the Rivers Thame and Isis on Henley Bridge are her work. Horace Walpole, her cousin, admired her enormously and left her his house, Strawberry Hill, in Twickenham. Unfortunately, Anne Damer ordered that all her correspondence and notes should be destroyed at her death – even more unfortunately, this was carried out. She was buried in Sundridge church, in Kent.

EMILY DAVIES

1830–1921
Plaque: 17 Cunningham Place, St John's Wood, NW8

Miss Davies' feminist views were formed as the result of her own experience and observation. She perceived that it was the common lot of girls like herself to stay at home and pick up such education and occupations as they could. (Barbara Stephen, 1927)

From the time when, as a young woman, she had encouraged her friend, Elizabeth Garrett (q.v.), to

become a doctor, to the day she saw a college for women established at Girton, Cambridge, Emily Davies was a passionate advocate of higher education for women. As one of the original founders of Girton College, there is a memorial to her in their chapel. She died at her home in Belsize Park, London.

CHRISTIAN, or CHRISTIANNA, DAVIS

1667–1739
(née Cavanagh)
Buried: Royal Hospital,
Chelsea, SW3 (unmarked)

Born in Dublin, Christian was seduced by a cousin and later married her aunt's servant, Richard Welch, who left home one day and failed to return. Almost a year passed before he wrote. He had, he said, got drunk, boarded a ship and found himself the next morning a recruit in His Majesty's army and bound for Holland. Christian cut her hair, disguised herself as a young man and enlisted as 'Christopher' Welch in a regiment also bound for Holland. Wounded at the battle of Landen, she retired to recuperate, rejoined her regiment, was taken prisoner by the French and then released on an exchange.

By this time, she was so carried away by her role that she is supposed to have fought a duel over a girl. Then another girl took a fancy to this handsome young soldier and, when her advances were rejected, accused him of being the father of the child she was expecting. Christian accepted paternity rather than be discovered!

When she finally caught up with her husband, he was involved with another woman, so they decided to remain just friends. However, Christian was severely wounded at the Battle of Ramillies, her real sex was discovered, and her husband claimed her. They were solemnly remarried, but he was then killed in action.

Christian returned to England and civilian life, ran a public-house for a while and married a soldier named Davis. She was finally received into Chelsea Hospital where she died and was buried.

EMILY DAVISON

1872–1913
Holloway Prison,
Parkhurst Road, N7

Emily once scrawled on the wall of her cell in Holloway Prison – 'Rebellion against tyrants is obedience to God'. Born at Blackheath, educated mainly in London, she finally took up teaching. In 1906, her interest aroused by attending meetings, Emily joined the Women's Social and Political Union (WSPU) and quickly became a militant campaigner for women's suffrage.

Frequent imprisonment for her part in demonstrations led to her joining the hunger strikes and, inevitably, to being forcibly fed. On one occasion in Holloway she barricaded herself into her cell; prison warders only broke in after hosing ice-cold water through the window. Imprisoned again, and horrified by the sufferings of fellow prisoners, Emily protested by hurling herself down a flight of stairs – she survived, although severely injured. The authorities had her forcibly fed again before she had fully recovered.

Emily seems not to have confided in any of her friends before leaving to attend the Derby in June 1913, but gave the impression of being cheerful and normal. She had wrapped the suffragette colours round herself under her coat and stood close to the rails. As the horses swept round Tattenham Corner she ran out onto the course and appeared to grasp the reins of the King's horse, Anmer; horse and jockey both fell. Emily Davison died a few hours later. Her protest was over. She is buried in Morpeth, Northumberland.

MARGARET DAMER DAWSON

1875–1920
Plaque: 10 Cheyne Row,
Chelsea, SW3

The daughter of Richard Dawson and Agnes, Lady Walsingham, Margaret Damer Dawson studied music and gained the gold medal

and diploma of the London Academy of Music. An energetic woman, she helped to organise the International Congress of Animal Protection Societies, held in London in 1906, but then became interested in the possibility of a women's police force. Having studied carefully the methods of those countries already using women in this capacity, she founded the Women Police Volunteers (which then became the Women's Police Service) in 1914.

> The Police authorities could give little or no help, more especially because war conditions made it impossible for them to give attention to the development of a new movement in police work. Everywhere we met the same question, 'What do you think you can do, ladies?' From the outset of our work in August 1914, we have eschewed voluntary service, and have demanded the recognition of the truth that the labourer is worthy of his hire. Thus the first British policewomen have started as professional officials, and it is from their work that the standard force of policewomen, with full powers and adequate pay, is being formed. (from an early report of the Women's Police Service)

She died, aged forty-five, at Lympne, in Kent, and was buried there.

NANCY DAWSON

d. 1767
Buried: St George's Gardens, Handel Street, WC1

Of all the girls in our town
The black, the fair, the red, the brown,
That dance and prance it up and down,
There's none like Nancy
    D*ws*n . . .

Born near Clare Market, Holborn, Nancy was taken on by a puppeteer as his assistant when she was sixteen. '. . . She danced, she tumbled, she sung and played upon the tabor and pipe . . .' – all with such *joie de vivre*, that she was noticed by one of the Sadlers Wells company, who offered her work. Later she appeared at Covent Garden, and it was in 1759 that her opportunity came: the man

who danced the hornpipe in *The Beggar's Opera* was unable to appear one night and Nancy replaced him at the last moment. She was electrifying: from then on the hornpipe became 'Miss Dawson's Hornpipe' and she became '. . . vastly celebrated, admired, imitated, and followed by everybody'.

Another of her talents was once delicately described as 'a natural inclination towards Beaus'. Rather less delicately:

> Now Nan was a free port of trade
> For every vessel to unlade:
> And whosoever came to her,
> French, Dutch, Italian, pimp or peer;

'Twas si Signor, 'twas yaw
mynheer,
'Twas si-vous-plait Monsieur.

**St George's Gardens,
WC1: somewhere here is
buried the 'vastly
celebrated' Nancy
Dawson**

Nancy seems to have retired
about four years before she died.
She was buried in the graveyard of
St George-the-Martyr, later known
as Bloomsbury Cemetery, and now

the delightful St George's Gardens
off Handel Street. Gravestones line
the walls, but if hers is one of them,
wind and rain have obliterated the
inscription: 'In Memory of the
Celebrated Nancy Dawson . . .'
(The rest is said to have been so
rude that it had to be removed.)

MARY DELANY

**1700–1788
(née Granville)
Buried: St James's,
Piccadilly, SW1**

A plaque in the north aisle of St
James's Church, Piccadilly,
commemorates the burial there of
Mrs Delany.

She seems to have positively
glowed with virtues and talent, but
her really remarkable achievement
was the *Flora* she began to compile
at the age of seventy-four. A
contemporary described her
method:

> . . . In the progress of her work, she
> pulls the flower in pieces, examines
> anatomically the structure of its
> leaves, stems, and buds; and having
> cut her papers to the shape of the
> several parts, she puts them
> together, giving them a richness and
> consistence, by laying one piece
> over another, and often a
> transparent piece over part of a
> shade, which softens it. Very rarely

she gives any colour with a brush.
She pastes them, as she works, upon
a black ground . . . These flowers
have both the beauty of painting
and the exactness of botany; and
the work, I have no doubt, into
whatever hands it may hereafter
fall, will be long considered as a
great curiosity.

Mary Delany had to give up her
absorbing task at the age of
eighty-three, as her eyesight was
failing – but by then she had
completed 980 plants and filled ten
volumes. In 1897 these were
bequeathed to the British Museum
by Lady Llanover.

CHARLOTTE DESPARD

1844–1939
(née French)
Nine Elms Lane, SW8

An ardent revolutionary, Charlotte Despard saw women's suffrage as only part of a far larger problem. Interviewed on her ninety-third birthday, she remarked that the feminist movement had not achieved all she had hoped for and that there was much left to be done, particularly regarding equal pay.

Born in Kent, she moved to London when she was eighteen, married, and after her husband's death served as a Poor Law Guardian at Kingston-upon-Thames. After this she lived at Nine Elms, where she opened one of the first child welfare centres and also ran a working-man's club. During the battle for women's votes she became President of the Women's Freedom League and

was imprisoned for militant activities. Mrs Despard was also one of those who refused to pay taxes, but, unlike many suffragettes who backed the war effort in 1914, she joined the Peace Movement.

After the war she lived in Ireland where she became an open supporter of Sinn Fein. Ironically, her brother was Lord Lieutenant of Ireland at the time. On one of her London visits, aged eighty-two, she joined the demonstration for equal franchise, and, at ninety, published her first volume of poetry.

'I cannot,' she observed, 'say whether my life has been successful . . . What I can say, though, is that it has been a happy one and never a dull one.'

CATHERINE DICKENS

1815–1879
(née Hogarth)
Buried: Highgate Cemetery (West), Swains Lane, N6

From the day she married Charles Dickens at St Luke's Church, Chelsea, to their separation over twenty years later Catherine, somehow, didn't stand a chance.

Early in the marriage her young sister Mary became part of the household and, unexpectedly, died. Dickens, overwhelmed with grief, ordered a double plot in

The grave of the Dickens family in Highgate Cemetery West

Catherine Dickens contd.

Kensal Green Cemetery where, he said, he wished to be buried at Mary's side.

Overwhelmed by constant pregnancies, a large family and a husband she couldn't understand, by 1851 Catherine was showing signs of nervous strain. Dickens became more and more irritated by her and another sister, Georgina, began to take over the running of their home. The situation rapidly deteriorated and, in 1857, aware

that Dickens was becoming involved with Ellen Ternan (q.v.), an actress, Catherine decided on a separation, which was settled the following year.

Catherine was given a house of her own, an annuity and her son Charles to stay with her. The rest of the children remained in the care of Georgina Hogarth and under Dickens's control. She lived in quiet bitterness near Regent's Park until her death.

JANE DIGBY
1807–1881
Married from her father's house in Harley Street, W1

A direct descendant of Sir Kenelm Digby and his wife (see Venetia Digby), Jane is said to have been a brilliant horsewoman and a good artist. She specialised, however, in falling in love with – and sometimes marrying – men.

When her family moved from Norfolk to London, Jane was introduced to 'society' and soon married Edward Law (Lord Ellenborough). Neglected by her husband, she began an affair with Prince Felix Schwarzenberg, an attaché at the Austrian Embassy. This led to a scandal, a debate in the House of Lords and a parliamentary divorce. Jane went abroad, gave birth to a daughter and, for a while, joined Prince Felix in Paris. There she met Balzac, who is said to have used her as the basis for the character of Lady Arabella Dudley in his novel *Le Lys dans La Vallée*.

Having quarrelled with Felix, Jane moved to Munich, became friendly with King Ludwig of

Bavaria and also began an affair with Baron Karl Venningen. She married the Baron and gave birth to a son, but soon found her attention distracted by the handsome Count Spiridon Theotoky of Corfu. Divorced from Venningen, she married the Count and lived with him on the island of Tinos, in Corfu, and also in Athens, where their son died in a tragic accident. The marriage began to deteriorate and Jane consoled herself for a while with a dashing brigand called Hajji Petros. This affair was a disappointment. Bored and disillusioned, she packed her bags and set off for Syria where, after various adventures, she met and, in 1854, married Medjuel, Sheikh of the Mezrab tribe.

'Jane Digby El Mezrab' led the life of a Bedouin wife and remained married to Medjuel. She died in Damascus and was buried in the Protestant cemetery there.

LADY VENETIA DIGBY
1600–1633
(née Stanley)
Buried: Christchurch, Newgate Street, EC1
(Church tower only left)

Sir Edward Stanley's gorgeous daughter Venetia, according to that delightful gossip John Aubrey, was hidden away in Oxfordshire to prevent her from getting into mischief. Reports of her beauty soon began to circulate, and when she was brought to London she became the mistress of the Duke of Dorset who paid her an annuity of five hundred pounds for the privilege.

Then another of her admirers, Sir Kenelm Digby, fell so desperately in love with her that he

actually married her – much against her mother's wishes – in 1625. Venetia gave birth to three sons, and then, very suddenly, died when she was only thirty-three (giving rise to the rumour that her husband had caused her death by dosing her with viper wine, to preserve her beauty!).

She was buried in Christchurch, Newgate. Sir Kenelm, it is said, never shaved again and several poets mourned her loss. Ben Jonson, in his incomplete *Eupheme, or the Fair Fame* left a slightly daunting portrait of her:

She had a mind as calm, as she was
   fair;
Not tossed or troubled with light
   Lady-air;
But, kept an even Gate, as some
   straight tree
Moved by the wind, so comely
   moved she.
And by the awful manage of her Eye

She swayed all Business in the
   Family.
To one, she said, Do this, he did it;
   So
To another, Move; he went; to a
   third, Go,
He run; and all did strive with
   diligence
T'obey and serve her sweet
   Commandements.

'JENNY DIVER'

Alias Mary Young alias Murphy alias Webb:

'The most noted pickpocket of her time'

approx 1705–1740
Buried: Old St Pancras
Church, NW1
(unmarked)

'What! And my pretty Jenny Diver too! As prim and demure as ever! There is not any prude, though ever so high bred has a more sanctified look with a more mischievous heart. Ah! Thou art a dear artful hypocrite.' (Macheath in *The Beggar's Opera*)

Within two years of her arrival in London, Jenny Diver had become the leader of a gang of thieves who would have followed her to the ends of the earth. Her cool nerve and sheer audacity were breath-taking, as when she adopted her favourite disguise:

Jenny had got two false arms made, and hands, by an ingenious artist, and dressing herself very genteely, like a citizen's wife, big with child with a pillow artfully fixed under her coats . . . and her arms fixed on, she hid her real ones under her petticoat, and the artificial ones came across her belly. Dressed in this condition, with one of her gang in the habit of a footman, she . . . goes to the meeting-house . . .
Now it was so ordered that our big-bellied lady was placed in a pew

between two elderly ladies, who had both repeating watches by their side; she sat very quietly all the time of the service, but at the conclusion of the last prayer, the audience being standing she took both the ladies' watches off, and tipped them to one of her companions . . . Now the congregation breaking up, every body was in a hurry to get out, and the gang surrounded the ladies in order to make a greater crowd, and help Jenny off if she should be discovered.

Although she was twice sentenced to transportation Jenny survived and was living in Wapping when she was caught for the third, and last, time. Tried at the Old Bailey, found guilty and sentenced to death, she was executed at Tyburn. Her enthusiastic biographer (the Chaplain of Newgate Prison at the time) recorded that 'she was buried on the Sunday following, in Pancrass churchyard'.

PHYLLIS DIXEY

1914–1964
(Mrs Tracy)
Whitehall Theatre,
Whitehall, SW1

Phyllis Dixey, Britain's most famous stripper and fan-dancer, particularly during the war years (1939–45), was once billed as 'The Girl the Lord Chamberlain Banned'. Her show, *Peek-A-Boo*, ran into trouble with various authorities while on tour. One magistrate cleared her of charges of appearing in an indecent show when told that she always appeared with her body covered in liquid silk.
   She married the comedian Jack Tracy in 1937. In 1944 she took over the lease of the Whitehall Theatre in London and it was there

she presented the highly successful farce *Worm's Eye View* which ran for 2,245 performances. In 1959 she was adjudged bankrupt, but two years later applied successfully for a discharge. Due to ill-health Phyllis Dixey had virtually retired by 1956. She died at her home in Epsom, Surrey.

LOTTIE (CHARLOTTE) DOD

1871–1960
Wimbledon, All England
Lawn Tennis Club, SW19

Lottie Dod won her first tennis singles title at Wimbledon in 1887. She was under sixteen at the time and defeated Miss Bingley (who was 'noted for her soft leather gauntlets and businesslike demeanour'). Lottie dominated the ladies' singles for seven years and then turned her attention to golf.

In 1904 she won the British Women's Golf Championship. She was also a champion skater, a hockey international and an excellent archer. She died at Sway, in Hampshire.

ELIZABETH DYSART

d. 1698
(Duchess of
Lauderdale)
Lived: Ham House,
Richmond, Surrey

Ham House, near Richmond, as one sees it today, preserves almost intact the taste of Elizabeth Dysart and her second husband, the Duke of Lauderdale. The property, which was Elizabeth's, was altered, re-decorated and re-furnished after their marriage in 1672. Countess of Dysart in her own right, Elizabeth's marriage to the Duke of Lauderdale made her one of the most powerful as well as one of the wealthiest women in England:

Ham House, near
Richmond, home of
Elizabeth Dysart

... She was a woman of great beauty, but of far greater parts; had a wonderful quickness of apprehension, and an amazing vivacity in conversation; had

studied not only divinity and history, but mathematics and philosophy; but, what ruined these accomplishments, she was restless in her ambition, profuse in her expense, and of a most ravenous covetousness; nor was there anything she stuck at to compass her end, for she was violent in everything – a violent friend, and a much more violent enemy . . .

Bishop Gilbert Burnet's assessment of her may be close to the truth. There is a fascinating portrait (by Lely) in Ham House of the Lauderdales in devastatingly confident middle age. Elizabeth was buried in Petersham Church, Surrey.

MARIA EDGEWORTH

1767–1849
Lambeth Palace, Lambeth Palace Road, SE1

Although much of her life was spent at home in Edgeworthstown (Longford, Ireland), Maria Edgeworth travelled extensively and frequently visited her friends in London.

A tiny woman – under four foot eight inches – she suffered from migraine, always thought herself ugly, and was convinced that she owed her success as a writer entirely to her father's influence. Her best known novels were *Castle Rackrent* (1800), and *Belinda* (1801), which was mentioned by Jane Austen in *Northanger Abbey*. She was considered a genius, fêted wherever she went, and, in her seventies, dined at Lambeth Palace seated at the right hand of the Archbishop of Canterbury.

Anne Thackeray Ritchie (q.v.) wrote of her:

> Whether . . . in some quiet Hampstead parlour talking to an old friend, or in her own home among books and relations . . . Miss Edgeworth seems to have been constantly the same, with presence of mind and presence of heart too, ready to respond to everything . . . 'I could not bear the idea that you suspected me of being so weak, so vain, so senseless,' she once wrote to Mrs Barbauld, 'as to have my head turned by a little fashionable flattery.' If her head was not turned it must have been because her spirit was stout enough to withstand the world's almost irresistible influence.

AMELIA BLANDFORD EDWARDS

1831–1892
The Egypt Exploration Society, 3 Doughty Mews, WC1

Amelia Edwards, successful journalist and novelist, was forty-three when she visited Egypt for the first time. A chance encounter with a stranger may change some lives; merely reading a certain book may change others. For Miss Edwards it was a casual change of plan in a travel itinerary. She wrote later:

> In simple truth we had drifted hither by accident, with no excuse of health, or business, or any serious object whatever: and had just taken refuge in Egypt as one might turn aside into the Burlington Arcade . . . to get out of the rain.

The experience was to have far-reaching results. She published *A Thousand Miles up the Nile* and, with Sir Erasmus Wilson, founded the Egypt Exploration Fund (now the Egypt Exploration Society) in 1882. When she died she left her library and collection of Egyptian antiquities to University College, London, together with enough money to establish the first Chair of Egyptology in Britain.

QUEEN ELEANOR

d. 1290
(of Castille)
Buried: Westminster Abbey;
Monument: outside Charing Cross Station, WC2

Eleanor was married to Edward I for over thirty years and was crowned in Westminster Abbey. Her son (Edward II) was made 'Prince of Wales', thus creating a precedent which survives to this day.

She accompanied her husband on his crusades, during which adventures she is said to have sucked poison from a wound made by his would-be assassin. Queen Eleanor died at Harby, in Nottinghamshire. Her body was transported from there to London, and memorial crosses were set up to mark the resting places on the journey; only those at Northampton, Geddington and Waltham remain. In London a Victorian-Gothic monument, outside Charing Cross Station, replaces the original 'Eleanor Cross' which commemorated the final stop before her burial in Westminster Abbey.

GEORGE ELIOT (MARY ANNE EVANS)

1819–1880
Buried: Highgate
Cemetery (East),
Swains Lane, N6

I'm not denyin' the women are
foolish: God Almighty made 'em to
match the men. (from *Adam Bede*)

Born near Nuneaton, Mary Anne
Evans left the Midlands after her
father's death and moved to
London in 1851. She became
assistant editor of the *Westminster
Review* and was introduced to
George Lewes, the writer, who had
been deserted by his wife. Breaking
the rigid social rules of the time,
she lived with him from 1854 until
his death in 1878.

Lewes encouraged her to write
fiction and, soon after the
publication of her *Scenes from
Clerical Life* (1858), she adopted
the pseudonym 'George Eliot',
writing in quick succession *Adam
Bede* (1859), *The Mill on the Floss*

(1860) and *Silas Marner* (1861). A
later novel, *Middlemarch* (1871)
was described by John Buchan as
'the greatest novel of the Victorian
age'. She was a serious woman and
a serious novelist, hoping not
merely to describe society, but to
change it. The plot of each of her
stories is carefully structured and
developed and her writing has a
fine tragic intensity.

Lonely and unhappy after
Lewes' death, she married an old
friend, John Walter Cross, in 1880,
but died the same year. In 1980, to
mark her centenary, a memorial
plaque was placed in the floor of
Poets' Corner, Westminster Abbey
and there is also a blue plaque on 4
Cheyne Walk, SW3, where she
lived for a short time.

George Eliot's tomb in
Highgate Cemetery East

QUEEN ELIZABETH I

1533–1603
Tomb: Westminster
Abbey;
Statue: St Dunstan's-
in-the-West, Fleet Street,
EC4

Daughter of Henry VIII and Anne
Boleyn, born at Greenwich, she
died at Richmond and was buried
in Westminster Abbey.

There will never Queen sit in my
seat with more zeal to my country,
care to my subjects, and that will
sooner with willingness venture her
life for your good and safety, than
myself. For it is my desire to live nor
reign no longer than my life and
reign shall be for your good. And
though you have had and may have

many princes more mighty and wise
sitting in this seat, yet you never had
nor shall have any that will be more
careful and loving. (November,
1601)

**Statue of Queen Elizabeth I in Fleet
Street**

RUTH ELLIS

1926–1955
(née Neilson)
The 'Magdala' pub, South
Hill Park, NW3

Ruth Ellis was the last woman to be hanged in Britain.

On 10 April, 1955 she shot Colin Blakeley, the man she loved, outside the Magdala pub near Hampstead Heath in London. On 21 June a jury at the Old Bailey found her guilty, with no recommendation for mercy. Her solicitor wrote to the Home Secretary explaining why he thought she should be reprieved, signatures were collected, petitions drawn up, investigations and reports continued. Ruth spent the time in the condemned cell making dolls, doing jig-saw puzzles, reading the Bible and chatting to visitors. She refused to say who had supplied the gun she had used or who had driven her to the Magdala pub.

When George Rogers, MP, visited her and persuaded her that she should put up a fight, for the sake of her young son, she allowed him to ask the Home Secretary for clemency. George Rogers was not granted an interview, and when Ruth finally signed a statement admitting who had helped her, the person in question could not be found in time. She was hanged at Holloway Prison on 13 July, and was buried there.

In August, 1955 the National Campaign for the Abolition of Capital Punishment was launched and in February the following year the Bill to abolish the death penalty was passed by the House of Commons. In 1965 the death penalty was suspended for five years. In 1969 it was abolished.

The remains of Ruth Ellis were re-buried at St Mary's, Amersham, in April 1971.

Magdala Tavern, Southill Park, Hampstead where Ruth Ellis shot Colin Blakeley

VIOLET VAN DER ELST

1882–1966
(née Dodge)
Lived: 4 Palace Gate, W8

I remember the words of Lord Bulwer Lytton, 'The greatest crime that man can do to man is to hang him.'

Violet Dodge was born in Feltham and went to school at what became Hanworth Road Junior School. Her first marriage, to Edward Nathan, ended when he died in 1927. Violet moved to 4 Palace Gate, Kensington, started a successful beauty business under the name of Sarah Brook, and married John Julien Van der Elst.

In 1934, Mr Van der Elst died and his wealthy widow became interested in the abolition of capital punishment. The first of her many, very personal, demonstrations took place outside Pentonville Prison before the execution of George Harvey. From that time on, there was no holding her. She organised petitions, hired sandwich-board men and loudspeakers, arrived herself outside prisons at the appropriate time, wearing black and in her

Rolls Royce – once she even hired planes to fly over Wandsworth Prison, trailing black flags behind them.

Interested in painting, spiritualism, music and dogs, her enthusiasm for the cause of abolition never waned. In 1955, then in her seventies, she protested over the execution of Ruth Ellis (q.v.). Mocked and held up to ridicule by her opponents, sniggered at for her eccentric methods, Violet Van der Elst was present in the gallery of the House of Commons when the first Bill to abolish the death penalty was passed in 1956.

ELIZABETH ELSTOB

1683–1756
St Margaret's Church, Westminster (no trace of grave)

For first, I know it will be said, What has a woman to do with learning? This I have known urged by some men, with an envy unbecoming that greatness of soul, which is said to dignify their sex.

With these words Elizabeth Elstob, linguist and scholar, defended herself in the preface to one of her books. Probably the first woman in England to study the Saxon language, she published *An English-Saxon Homily on the Day of Saint Gregory* in 1709 and an *English-Saxon Grammar* in 1715. She was working on the homilies of Aelfric when her brother, with whom she lived in the City of London, died and Elizabeth, in severe financial difficulty, had to leave. Moving to Worcestershire, she ran a small school in Evesham single-handed, in an attempt to earn her living with, as she remarked, 'very indifferent success'. At last an annuity was raised for her, she was able to afford a helper and so continue her

studies. To her great pleasure she also met a kindred spirit, George Ballard of Magdalen College, Oxford (later the author of *Memoirs of British Ladies, who have been celebrated by their writings or skill etc.*) with whom she corresponded regularly.

Elizabeth finally became governess to the Duchess of Portland's children, a position she held until her death. It is said she was buried in the church of St Margaret's, Westminster.

DAME EDITH EVANS

1888–1976
(Mrs Booth)
Lived: Ebury Street, SW1

Edith Evans, born in Pimlico, London, was apprenticed to a milliner when she left school. She became one of the outstanding actresses of the twentieth century and will long be remembered for the style and brilliance of her performances, especially in comedy.

The ideal Lady Bracknell in Oscar Wilde's *The Importance of Being Earnest* ('. . . a *hand*-bag?'), she triumphed as Rosalind, in *As You Like It*, Madame Ranevsky in *The Cherry Orchard*, Mrs St Maugham in *The Chalk Garden*, and perhaps especially as the nurse in *Romeo and Juliet*. In 1925 she married Guy Booth, whom she had known for many years.

Dame Edith Evans died at her home in Kent, but her memorial service was held in the 'actors' church, St Paul's, Covent Garden.

DAME MILLICENT GARRETT FAWCETT

1847–1929
(née Garrett)
Plaque: 2 Gower Street, WC1;
Memorial: Westminster Abbey Chapel of the Holy Cross.

I cannot recall any other occasion on which the illness of an elderly lady of no official rank has caused so much affectionate concern as to necessitate the posting of a bulletin on her door, but there have been so many callers at Dame Millicent Fawcett's house that it has been impossible to cope with their inquiries in any other way.

Dame Millicent still keeps house in Bloomsbury . . . for she remains closely in touch with London affairs and was present at the luncheon to the women members of Parliament less than a week ago. (*The London Evening Standard*, 31 July 1929)

A week later Dame Millicent Fawcett was dead. One of the leading figures in the women's suffrage movement for more than fifty years, she was one of the few who lived long enough to see the battle won for, in 1928, aged eighty-one, she was in the House of Lords to hear the assent given to a Bill allowing women equal voting rights with men.

Her blind husband, Henry Fawcett, was Professor of Political Economy at Cambridge. They both worked hard for the extension of university education for women and, in 1890, their daughter Philippa (q.v.) gained 400 marks above the nearest male contender in the mathematical tripos of that year at Cambridge.

Dame Millicent Fawcett was the leader of the constitutional wing of the suffrage movement and did not approve of militant tactics. Nevertheless she fought fiercely in her own way and it is said that her favourite quotation was the message General Foch is supposed to have sent to General Joffre during the Battle of the Marne:

> My centre is giving way; my right is falling back; situation excellent; I attack.

Millicent Garrett Fawcett's house in Gower Street, WC1

PHILIPPA GARRETT FAWCETT

1868–1948
County Hall (now headquarters of the Greater London Council) Westminster Bridge Road, SE1

In 1890, Philippa Fawcett made history at Cambridge when she was classed 'above senior wrangler' in the mathematical tripos. As a woman she was denied the coveted title, but nothing could destroy her victory, which was celebrated at Newnham, her college, with dancing, singing and fireworks. The heroine was chaired three times round a bonfire in the grounds.

The only child of Millicent Garrett Fawcett (q.v.), the suffragette leader, and Henry Fawcett, the blind Postmaster-General, Philippa later became private secretary to the acting Director of Education in South Africa and helped to establish public elementary education in the Transvaal. In 1905 she was made Principal Assistant in the Education Department of the London County Council, County Hall and, in 1920, appointed Assistant Education Officer, a post she held until her retirement.

SOPHIE FEDOR-OVITCH

1893–1953
Plaque: St Paul's Church, Covent Garden, WC2

Born in Russia, Sophie Fedorovitch came to England in 1920. A stage designer, she worked with most of the leading ballet companies, including the Sadlers Wells, and in close collaboration with Frederick Ashton and Marie Rambert. Her trade-mark was elegant simplicity, combined with clever lighting and an uncluttered stage. She died in London and her memorial plaque in St Paul's Church, Covent Garden, includes these lines:

> Loveliness was more resplendent made
> By the mere passing of that cavalcade
> With plumes and cloaks and housings . . .
> (Longfellow)

LAVINIA FENTON

1708–1760
(Duchess of Bolton)
Buried: St Alphege Church, Greenwich, SE10

Born in London and brought up in an eighteenth-century coffee-house owned by her mother and step-father, Lavinia soon won admiration for her charm, her musical ability and her looks. In 1726 she made her first stage appearance and, two years later, was cast as Polly Peachum in John Gay's *Beggar's Opera*. She immediately became the toast of the town:

> My heart was so free,
> It roved like the bee,
> Till Polly my passion requited;
> I sipt each flower,
> I chang'd every hour,
> But here ev'ry flow'r is united.
> (Sung by Macheath in *The Beggar's Opera*)

She attracted the attention of the Duke of Bolton and became his mistress. Much later (when his wife died) he married her or, as Mrs Inchbald, in her introduction to an edition of *The Beggar's Opera*, elegantly put it:

> Miss Fenton, the original Polly, so fascinated the Duke of Bolton, that he elevated her to the highest rank of a female subject, by making her his wife.

A painting by Hogarth (Tate Gallery), shows her in the role of Polly, with the Duke watching from the audience.

KATHLEEN FERRIER

1912–1953
Plaque: 97 Frognal, Hampstead, NW3

I made my London debut a week last Monday at the National Gallery and oh boy! Did my knees knock!

Kathleen Ferrier was born in Lancashire. When she left school at the age of fourteen, to work in the Post Office, she was already a talented pianist. Two years later she won the North-regional contest in a piano-playing competition, organised by the *Daily Express* newspaper. Gradually her interest in music began to veer towards singing; she took lessons and developed the rich, full contralto that eventually made her famous.

In 1935 she married a Mr Wilson, but the marriage was a failure and was annulled in 1947.

During the Second World War

she toured for CEMA (Council for the Encouragement of Music and the Arts), singing in halls, schools and churches. By 1943 she had moved to London where she lived in Hampstead with her father and her sister Winifred. That year she also sang the alto part in Handel's *Messiah* at Westminster Abbey.

> If anyone had told me when I was twenty that at thirty-two I should be dashing about the country singing at concerts, I should have laughed my head off. I should have said that no one could make a career in music without going to the Royal Academy or the Royal College, and anyway that it was much too risky a way of earning a living.

Kathleen Ferrier sang Lucretia in Benjamin Britten's opera, *The Rape of Lucretia*, at Glyndebourne in 1946 and performed there again in Gluck's *Orfeo* the following year. She travelled extensively, singing in Holland, Sweden, Austria and America – but her time was rapidly running out. In February 1953, singing once more in *Orfeo* at Covent Garden Opera House, she collapsed at the end of the second performance and died of cancer eight months later.

The 'Kathleen Ferrier Memorial Scholarship' and the 'Kathleen Ferrier Cancer Research Fund' were founded in her memory. There is a plaque to her in the waiting-room of the Radiotherapy Department of University College Hospital in London.

CELIA FIENNES
1662–1741
Hyde Park

After a prolonged illness, Celia Fiennes, granddaughter of the first Viscount Saye and Sele, decided that travel would improve her health. She explored much of England on horseback, making detailed notes, and left a fascinating account of English life in the late seventeenth century. A part of London that she noticed particularly was Hyde Park:

> which is for riding on horseback but mostly for the coaches, there being a Ring railed in, round which a gravel way that would admitt of twelve if not more rowes of coaches, which the Gentry to take aire and see each other comes and drives round and round.

She lived for a while in Barnet and died at Hackney but was buried at Newton Toney, in Wiltshire.

DOROTHEA WOODWARD FISHER
1894–1974
Narrow Street, E14

> I reckon a woman has to work for respect. I never met any prejudice on the river. But I have a gruff voice and I can be as tough as any man.

Educated at Cheltenham Ladies College, Dorothea Woodward, ignoring her family's advice, married Bill Fisher, a London lighterman. With twenty pounds and an old barge, the Fishers began a business that became one of the largest barge fleets on the Thames, with headquarters in Limehouse.

Mrs Fisher ran the fleet herself after her husband's death, directing operations from her home in Lewisham, but vast changes in the Inner London docks affected the lighterage business. In 1972, when she was seventy-eight, Woodward Fisher Ltd., Lightermen, Tug Owners (Barge Repairs) finally closed down.

Known familiarly as 'Ma Thames', Dorothea Woodward Fisher had become one of the best-known and most colourful figures in London's dockland. Wearing her Savile Row suit (a tailored jacket and skirt), she sported a monocle, smoked incessantly, and often went around with a parrot perched on her shoulder.

She was awarded the OBE for her generous work for charity, and at her funeral in Lewisham the escort for her coffin was provided by the Barge Master of the Fishmongers' Company and the Barge Master and Watermen of the Company of Watermen and Lightermen.

KITTY (CATHERINE) FISHER

?–1767
Gough Square, off Fleet Street (Dr Johnson's House), EC4

The mistress of several eminent men, Kitty was also an excellent horsewoman, a target for satirists and the model for many artists. She once called on Dr Johnson, but alas he was not at home.

She *may* be the heroine of the rhyme:

Lucy Locket lost her pocket,
Kitty Fisher found it.
Not a penny was there in it,
But a ribbon round it.

Kitty finally married a Mr Norris. When she died she was buried at Benenden, in Kent.

MARY FITTON

1578–1647
Hampton Court Palace, Hampton Court, Kingston-upon-Thames

Mary Fitton may have been Shakespeare's 'dark lady' of his sonnets. She arrived in London in 1595 as maid of honour to Elizabeth I. There she met William Herbert (Earl of Pembroke and one of Shakespeare's patrons) and fell in love. Mary comes vividly to life in a contemporary description:

> When that Mrs Fitton was in great favour . . . and during the time that the Earl of Pembroke favoured her, she would put off her head Tire and tuck up her clothes and take a large white cloak, and march as though she had been a man to meet the said Earl out of the court.

However, when she became pregnant, and William Herbert refused to marry her, Mary was disgraced and left the court. She stayed for a while with her sister Anne at Arbury Hall, Warwickshire and then married a Captain Polwhele in 1607. Mary later survived a second husband and was buried at her birth-place, Gawsworth in Cheshire.

MARY ANN FLAXMAN

1768–1833
Buried: Old St Pancras Church, NW1 (unmarked)

Mary Ann lived in the shadow of her brilliant elder brother, the sculptor and illustrator, John Flaxman. She worked for some years as a governess, but then became an artist in her own right. In 1803 William Hayley's poem *The Triumphs of Temper* was published, with six illustrations by Mary Flaxman (engraved by William Blake). From 1810 she lived with her brother and his wife in Buckingham Street, near Charing Cross, and at her death was buried with them in St Pancras Old Church graveyard.

ELIZA FLOWER

1803–1846
The Chapel, in South Place, Finsbury Square, EC2, destroyed during the Second World War

She sang much and often, because she loved it, because, as she said, she could not help it . . . She sang to the nurse's children, she sang as she went up and down stairs; she sang when she was glad, and when she was sorry.

After their father's death (their mother had died many years before) Eliza Flower and her sister Sarah moved into the home of their father's friend, William Fox, the Non-Conformist teacher, reformer and preacher. Fox was unhappily married, he and his wife barely on speaking terms, and Eliza began to work as his secretary. She also composed music: her *Fourteen Musical Illustrations of the Waverley Novels* was published in 1831. She delighted in setting words to music and did so for her sister's *Nearer my God to Thee*. Her most important work was *Hymns and Anthems: The Words Chiefly from the Holy Scripture and the Writings of the Poets*.

All went well, until her sister married and left. Mrs Fox, jealous of the developing affection between her husband and Eliza, complained. Mr and Mrs Fox agreed to live separate lives under the same roof, but Mrs Fox went further and made a more public complaint, to the congregation of her husband's chapel in Finsbury Square. Fox resigned, was persuaded to return, but the scandal finally resulted in a formal separation. Eliza and William Fox moved out, with two of his children, and they lived together until Eliza's death. She died of consumption at the age of forty-three and was buried with her father at Harlow in Essex.

DAME AGNES FORSTER

fl. 1454
Site of old Ludgate Prison,
Ludgate Hill, EC4

Ludgate prison, 'for those convicted for debt, trespass, accounts and contempts', no longer exists. Luckily John Stow, the sixteenth century London historian, noted 'certain verses graven in copper' and fixed to the wall, before they disappeared with the building:

> Devout souls that pass this way,
> For Stephen Forster, late mayor,
>   heartily pray:
> And Dame Agnes his spouse to God
>   consecrate,
> That of pity this house made for
>   Londoners in Ludgate.
> So that for lodging and water
>   prisoners here nought pay,
> As their keepers shall answer at
>   dreadful doomsday.

Dame Agnes not only ensured that the prisoners were given free lodging and water but also paid for enlarging and improving the building, to include an area where they could take fresh air and exercise. Most of this was done in memory of her husband, Stephen, whom, it is said, she first saw when he was himself a prisoner there. A wealthy widow, she paid for his release and then married him. In 1454 he became Lord Mayor of London.

Dame Agnes Forster was buried with her husband in the church of St Botolph's, Billingsgate, which was later destroyed by fire.

MARY FRITH ('MOLL CUTPURSE')

d. 1650
St Bride's Church, Fleet Street, EC4 (no trace of grave)

She was born . . . in Barbican, at the upper end of Aldersgate Street. A very tomrig or rumpscuttle she was . . .

The daughter of a shoemaker, Mary rebelled from an early age against the role expected of her.

> She could not endure that sedentary life of sewing or stitching, a Sampler was as grievous as a Winding-sheet, her Needle, Bodkin and Thimble, she could not think on quietly, wishing them changed into sword and Dagger for a bout at Cudgels . . .

Later she became 'Moll Cutpurse', a notorious, colourful and violent member of the Elizabethan underworld, swaggering in men's clothes, fighting, stealing, drinking and, it is said, practising a little highway robbery on the side. When Middleton and Dekker wrote a play based on her life they called it *The Roaring Girl*.

She died of dropsy and was buried in St Bridget's church, [now St Bride's]. The will left by this fairly unrepentant criminal ended with these words:

> Let me by lay'n in my Grave on my Belly, with my Breech upwards, as well for a lucky Resurrection at Doomsday, as because I am unworthy to look upwards, and that as I have in my LIFE been preposterous, so I may be in my Death; I expect not, nor will I purchase a Funeral Commendation; but if Mr H – be Squemish and will not Preach, let the Sexton mumble Two or Three Dusty Claiy words and put me in, and there's an End. (Quotes from *The Life and Death of Mrs Mary Frith etc.*, 1662)

ELIZABETH FRY

1780–1845
(née Gurney)
Plaque: St Mildred's Court, Poultry, EC2;
Statue: Central Criminal Court, Old Bailey, EC4 (not open to the public)

In the main entrance-hall of the Central Criminal Court (the 'Old Bailey') in London, stands a statue of Elizabeth Fry, Quaker and prison reformer. The inscription on the pedestal reads:

> One who never turned her back,
> But marched breast forward,
> Never doubted clouds would break,
> Never dreamed, though right were
>   worsted,
>   Wrong would triumph.

> Held, we fall to rise, are baffled to
>   fight better,
>   Sleep to wake.
>   (Robert Browning)

Elizabeth was born in Norwich and her mother died when she was twelve. A shy girl, she persuaded her father to take her to see the local 'House of Correction' for women, and then, having heard the American, William Savery, preach, she decided to become a Quaker.

Statue of Elizabeth Fry in the Old Bailey, EC4

In 1800 she married Joseph Fry. They lived in St Mildred's Court in the City of London, began to produce a large family (eventually sixteen children), and later moved to Plashet, in Essex.

Elizabeth was asked to visit Newgate Prison in London in 1813. She found over 800 prisoners crammed into a space designed for 500. They had no coal, no candles and little bedding. Children were herded together with hardened criminals and prisoners with money could buy as much drink as they could afford. Horrified, Elizabeth went home, organised her family and returned to Newgate in 1817. Establishing a school there for the children, she formed a group of women prisoners into a committee and began her programme of reform. When the city magistrates told her

that it was useless to expect any good results, she replied, 'Let the experiment be tried.'

Between 1818 and 1841 Elizabeth Fry cared for the condemned, held prayer meetings, visited almost every ship that sailed with women prisoners for Botany Bay and also began to fight capital punishment for theft. Gradually her methods began to attract attention abroad as well as in Britain and visiting groups were set up in France, Holland, Belgium and Germany.

The strain of family life and work began to affect her health. When she died, aged sixty-five, her last words are said to have been, 'Oh, my dear Lord help and keep thy servant'. She was buried in the Friends' burial-ground at Barking in Essex.

DAME KATHERINE FURSE

1875–1952
(née Symonds)
Lived: Sloane Court, SW3

Katherine married the painter C. W. Furse in 1900. He died four years later, leaving her with two young sons to bring up. She enrolled in one of the early Red Cross Voluntary Aid Detachments (VAD) and, in 1914, led the first official VAD unit to be sent abroad, where their job was to establish rest stations along the lines of communication. Later she organised a VAD Department in London and was decorated with the Royal Red Cross. Resigning in 1917, she was immediately offered the post of director of the new Women's Royal Naval Service.

After the war, she joined the Harry Lunn travel agency, and, an excellent skier herself, became the representative of the Ski Club of Great Britain in Switzerland. Her many other interests included the Girl Guide movement. Katherine was born in Bristol and died in London.

MARGUERITE GARDINER

1789–1849
(Countess of Blessington)
(née Power)
Site of Gore House:
Kensington Gore, SW7

Marguerite was born in Ireland. Married when she was under fifteen years of age to a Captain Farmer of the 47th Regiment, who treated her abominably, she ran away with a Captain Jenkins. Later, arriving in London under her lover's protection, she divided her affection between him and the wealthy Earl of Blessington, a widower. When her husband died and Jenkins immediately proposed marriage, Marguerite, according to her obituary in the *Gentleman's Magazine* of 1849, told the Earl that:

> She would prefer being made a lady as well as merely an honest woman, and the easy-going peer made her both, presenting her with a ring and a coronet at one and the same time.

In 1822 Marguerite, now Lady Blessington, published (anonymously) her first book, *The Magic Lantern, or Sketches of Scenes in the Metropolis*. After this she wrote continuously, travel books, novels and magazine articles, later editing *The Keepsake and Book of Beauty* for many years. She met Lord Byron and wrote about their friendship in her *Conversations*, which was first published in the *New Monthly Magazine*.

Before her husband's death, while living in Paris, she became involved with the Count d'Orsay, a colourful society figure (see Jane Welsh Carlyle). After her husband's death she returned to London and moved into Gore House, Kensington (the Albert Hall now stands on the site) and became a brilliant hostess:

> Her house at Kensington Gore was for fourteen years the resort of the most distinguished men of wit and genius of every country and opinion. (*Gentleman's Magazine*, 1849)

In 1848, almost bankrupt, she sold the house and moved to Paris where she died a year later. She was buried at Chambourcy, near St Germain-en-Laye.

ELIZABETH GASKELL

1810–1865
(née Stevenson)
Plaque: 93 Cheyne Walk, SW3

> In the first place, Cranford is in possession of the Amazons; all the holders of houses above a certain rent are women. If a married couple come to settle in the town, somehow the gentleman disappears; he is either fairly frightened to death by being the only man in the Cranford evening parties, or he is accounted for by being with his regiment, his ship, or closely engaged in business all the week in the great neighbouring commercial town of Drumble.
> (*Cranford*, 1853)

Elizabeth was born in Chelsea but her mother died soon afterwards and, only a year old, she was sent to live with her aunt in Cheshire. In 1832 she married the Rev. William Gaskell and they moved to Manchester, living there for the next forty years.

Elizabeth had four children but her only son died while still a baby. Hoping for a distraction from her intense grief she began to write. In her first novel, *Mary Barton*

(1848), she observed with sincerity and sympathy the effect of the Industrial Revolution on the lives of the ordinary people around her. She wrote to the end of her life, producing twelve volumes of stories, including the delightful portrait of village life, *Cranford* (1853) and also her sensitive *Life of Charlotte Brontë* (1857) (q.v.).

CATHERINE GLADSTONE

d. 1900
(née Glynne)
Plaque: 11 Carlton House Terrace, SW1

Catherine Gladstone: lived at 11 Carlton House Terrace, SW1

A deranging incident has occurred. I am engaged to be married. (William Gladstone to a friend)

Having been through the unpleasant experience of being jilted, Catherine Glynne was wary of young William Gladstone's overtures. However, he persevered and she accepted him at a garden party in Fulham. They were married in 1839 and after the honeymoon moved into their home at Carlton House Terrace, London. For the next fifty-eight years Catherine supported her husband through the varying fortunes of his political career. She also had eight children.

Gladstone told his wife everything; she not only knew about his mission to rescue prostitutes – highly unconventional at the time – but helped at every stage, receiving those who came home with him and working for their rehabilitation. A woman who made, and kept, many friends, she managed to remain popular with Queen Victoria even when Gladstone was definitely out of favour.

Catherine is buried in Westminster Abbey near her husband.

ELEANOR, DUCHESS OF GLOUCESTER

? –1457?
(née Cobham)
Westminster Abbey, SW1

'Stand forth, Dame Eleanor Cobham, Gloucester's wife:
In sight of God and us, your guilt is great.'
(Shakespeare, *Henry VI, Part Two*)

Tried (with others) for conspiring to bring about the death of Henry VI, among the charges brought against Eleanor Cobham was that of witchcraft, including the burning of the King's image in wax.

Mistress of Humphrey, Duke of Gloucester, the King's uncle, she became his wife in about 1428.

People dabbled in the 'Black Arts' in those days and Eleanor was probably no exception, but she was also suspected of being highly ambitious for her husband. In 1441, warned that members of her household had been arrested, she fled to Westminster Abbey for sanctuary. Examined by a panel of Archbishops and Bishops she maintained her innocence but, the next day, faced with an accomplice who had pleaded guilty, she admitted to some of the charges.

Of the accused, Eleanor alone

escaped the death penalty. Her humiliating penance was to walk through London streets on three separate market-days, wearing a sheet and carrying a candle; she was then banished. Moved from castle to castle, Eleanor was finally transferred to the Isle of Wight in 1446 and probably died there about ten years later.

ELINOR GLYN

1864–1943
(née Sutherland)
Married: St George's, Hanover Square, W1;
Lived: Shepherd Market, W1

Would you like to sin
With Elinor Glyn
On a tiger-skin?
Or would you prefer
    To err
    With her
On some other fur?

Elinor, married to Clayton Glyn at St George's Church, Hanover Square, London, wrote her first book, *The Visits of Elizabeth*, while recovering from rheumatic fever. She graduated to novels of high romance, and her *Three Weeks*, published in 1907, throbbed with passion, red roses – and tiger-skins. Mocked by the critics and banned at Eton, it sold in vast quantities.

After her husband's death, Elinor worked in Hollywood as a scriptwriter. She supervised the filming of *Three Weeks* in 1923, and another of her novels, *His Hour*, the following year. She returned to England in 1929 and lived finally in Shepherd Market, Mayfair.

ARABELLA GODDARD

1836–1922
(Mrs Davison)
Her Majesty's Theatre, Haymarket, SW1

Arabella, a child prodigy, played the piano at the age of seven, it is said, in the presence of Chopin. When she was fourteen she made her first public appearance as a concert pianist at Her Majesty's Theatre in London. Later, she married J. W. Davison, the critic, who had helped to train and advise her, and travelled extensively, playing in America, Australia and India. One of the first pianists to play by memory, she was also one of the first to play Beethoven's late sonatas in public.

MARGARET GODOLPHIN

1652–1678
(née Blagge)
Married: Temple Church, Temple Lane (Inner Temple), EC4

She contemplated for some time the freedom offered her in a remote hermitage vowed to perpetual celibacy . . . (*The Life of Mrs Godolphin* by John Evelyn)

In 1666, the year of the Great Fire of London, Margaret Blagge became a maid of honour to the Duchess of York. Charles II was on the throne, society was permissive, morals had relaxed, the court fluttered with frivolity. Margaret, against all odds, developed into a serious, virtuous and deeply religious young woman. Her friend and admirer, John Evelyn, the diarist, remembered her vowing: 'Be sure never to speak to the King when they speak filthily, tho' I be laughed at . . .'

Then she met Sidney Godolphin, Envoy Extraordinary to the French court. In 1675, after a great struggle between earthly love and the religious life, she married him at the Temple Church in the City of London. They moved into an apartment in Scotland Yard and Margaret was later delighted to find herself pregnant. In 1678, after giving birth to a son, Francis, she died of puerperal fever and was buried in the Godolphin Chapel, Breage Church, Cornwall.

JULIA GOODMAN

1812–1906
(née Salaman)
Buried: West London
Synagogue Cemetery,
Golders Green, NW11

· Julia Salaman received her education at a well-known school kept in Islington . . . There she was taught the piano and harp, in which she made no inconsiderable progress. But her inclination was for art, and upon leaving school she entered for a short time the drawing academy of Mr Sass, where Millais and Frith studied, and she received private lessons in painting from Robert Faulkner, a pupil of Reynolds. (*The Jewish Chronicle*, January, 1907)

In 1836 Julia married Louis Goodman, a city merchant. Previously she had copied old masters at the British Institution in Pall Mall so successfully that Samuel Rogers, owner of an original, once said, 'I really don't know which is my picture and which is Miss Salaman's copy.' After her marriage she began to specialise in portraits and, in 1838, her work was first exhibited at the Royal Academy. Later she was able to support an invalid husband and seven children on her commissions. She completed, it is said, more than a thousand portraits in oils and pastels.

CHRISTINE GRANVILLE

1915–1952
(née Skarbek)
Buried: Kensal Green
(Roman Catholic)
Cemetery, NW10

Dennis George Muldowney, aged 41, a porter at the Reform Club Pall Mall SW was charged with the murder of Christine Granville . . . at Lexham Gardens Kensington on Sunday . . . (*The Times*, 17th June 1952)

Polish by birth, Christine and her husband George Gizycki were in East Africa when war broke out in 1939. They immediately went to London. Christine was sent on a mission to Poland, where she helped to establish an escape route for Poles and British Prisoners-of-War. She was arrested twice, but released, and then reported to Cairo where she learned to become a radio operator. As a member of the Special Operations Executive she was parachuted into France in 1944 and worked there with the Maquis (the French Resistance). In one of her exploits, she released three fellow-agents who had been condemned to death. She was awarded the George Medal, OBE and Croix de Guerre.

After the war Christine became a British subject and took the name of Granville. Finding it difficult to settle, she worked as a switchboard operator, sold dresses at Harrods and became a stewardess on a liner. It was then she met Dennis Muldowney, who was working as a steward, and befriended him. Unstable and, it is said, a schizophrenic, he took a job at the Reform Club in London and waited for her one evening in the foyer of the Kensington hotel where she stayed between voyages. He stabbed her to death.

KATE GREENAWAY

1846–1901

Plaque: 39 Frognal,
Hampstead, NW3

Gravestone in Hampstead
Cemetery, NW6
'What beauteous land
may I be wandering in,
While you stand gazing at
what once was I?'

Pinafores, bonnets, children,
flowers, frills, smocks, sashes –
innocence . . . The Kate
Greenaway style survives in
greetings cards, birthday books,
friezes for bedroom walls and in
the nostalgia of Laura Ashley
dresses.

Born in Hoxton, London, Kate
took art classes in Clerkenwell and
then attended the new Slade School
of Art. In 1878 her first book,
Under the Window, was
published; hard on its heels was
the *Birthday Book for Children*.
Consistently popular, her work
was rarely criticised, although,
when she entered a drawing called
Misses to the Royal Academy, one
periodical could not resist the
temptation:

A picture by Miss Greenaway (we
  scarcely like a bit of it)
Is rightly titled *Misses*, for she
  hasn't made a hit of it.

Shy, serious, a perfectionist
('What a great pity my hands are
not clever enough to do what my
mind and eyes see, but there it is!'),
she made many friends and
corresponded for twenty years
with John Ruskin, the art critic.

In 1885 she moved, with her
parents and her brother, to a house
designed for her by Norman Shaw:
39 Frognal, Hampstead, and there
she died, her ashes quietly interred
in Highgate Cemetery.

What beauteous land may I be
  wandering in
While you stand gazing at what
  once was I?
Why, I may be to gold harps
  listening
And plucking flowers of
  immortality –
Why, Heaven's blue skies may shine
  above my head
While you stand there – and say
  that I am dead.

Kate Greenaway's home at 39 Frognal, Hampstead, designed by Norman Shaw

LADY JANE GREY

1537–1554
Executed: Tower of London, EC3

Then tied she the handkerchief about her eyes, and feeling for the block, she said, 'What shall I do? Where is it?' One of the standers-by guiding her thereunto she laid her head down upon the block, and then stretched forth her body, and said 'Lord, into thy hands I commend my spirit.'

Jane died, aged seventeen, on the scaffold in the Tower of London, a victim of power politics. Her father-in-law, the Duke of Northumberland, to further his own ambitions, had persuaded the dying young Edward VI to leave the crown not to either of his sisters, Mary and Elizabeth, but to Lady Jane and her male heirs. When Edward died, Jane, unwilling but trapped and helpless, was proclaimed Queen. Nine days later her reign was over and Northumberland's plot had failed. Mary was now Queen of England. Jane was moved to the Gentleman-Gaoler's lodgings in the Tower and kept in confinement for six months before her trial. She believed she would be pardoned, but, when offered a pardon on condition that she became a Catholic, she refused.

It has been recorded that she occupied some of the time by 'pricking' verses onto paper with a pin. One of them reads:

> 'While God assists us, envy bites in vain.
> If God forsake us; fruitless all our pain.
> I hope for light after this darkness . . .'

She was buried in the Tower church of St Peter ad Vincula. John Foxe, in his *Acts and Monuments* (1563), described the fate of one of her judges:

> Here is to be noted, that the Judge Morgan, who gave the sentence of condemnation against her, shortly after he had condemned her, fell mad, and in his raving cried out continually to have the Lady Jane taken away from him; and so ended his life.

LADY CHARLOTTE GUEST

1812–1895
(later Schreiber)
(née Bertie)
Lived: Cavendish Square, W1

When Lady Charlotte Schreiber died at her son's home, Canford Manor in Dorset, most obituaries mentioned that she had been a dedicated collector of old china, English painted fans and playing cards of all nations. Her first husband, Josiah John Guest, owned iron works in Dowlais, South Wales, and some of the obituaries referred to her management of the works after his death. *The Times* (1895) also remarked upon her knitting:

> During the last few years of her life, Lady Charlotte Schreiber was blind, yet she was able to knit, and she devoted a great part of her time to making woollen comforters, which were distributed amongst cab drivers at the end of each year.

No one seemed interested in the fact that, after her first marriage, and while living in Wales, Lady Charlotte had not only learned Welsh, but had also translated *The Red Book of Hergest* and the *Hanes Taliesin* (heroic tales of legendary Welsh heroes). The title she gave to her translation was *The Mabinogion*. It took her nearly eight years and was published in three volumes (1838–49). She also spent some of her time producing children – ten altogether.

There is no recorded earlier translation of the complete tales, although Dr Owen Pughe had translated some parts of them. Lady Charlotte's son later described the reaction of Lord Alfred Tennyson, the poet, to *The Mabinogion*:

> Lord Tennyson told one of my sisters that it was the first book he read after his marriage, and that he was so struck with it that it inspired him to write his poem. [The poem in question being Tennyson's *Idylls of the King*.]

After her second marriage to Charles Schreiber MP, in 1855, Lady Charlotte spent more of her time in London, and lived in Cavendish Square before moving finally to Dorset.

NELL (ELLEN) GWYNN

d. 1687
Buried: St Martin-in-the-Fields, Trafalgar Square, WC2 (no trace)

A block of flats in Sloane Avenue, SW3 bearing Nell Gwynn's name

. . . You never appear but you gladden the hearts of all that have the happy fortune to see you, as if you were made on purpose to put the whole world into good humour. (Dedication in Aphra Behn's *The Feigned Courtezans*)

Nell was brought up as a child in Coal Yard Alley, near Drury Lane, in London. She is supposed to have sold fish in the streets, worked as a servant-girl in a brothel and finally became an 'orange-girl', selling oranges to theatre audiences.

It was while she was the mistress of Charles Hart, an actor, that she learnt to sing, dance and act, making her first appearance on stage in 1664. For a short while she was the mistress of Lord Buckhurst, but Charles II soon began to show an interest in 'pretty, witty Nell'. She took up the challenge, bore him a son and moved into a grand house in Pall Mall.

Nell Gwynn was renowned for her figure, her honesty, her vulgarity, her lack of greed and her sense of humour. One of the few people she disliked was Louise de Kerouaille, another of Charles's mistresses, a foreigner and a Catholic. Louise was not popular with the public and one of the best-known stories about Nell concerns an occasion when her carriage was mobbed by a hostile crowd, who believed that Louise was inside. Nell, losing patience, stuck her head out of the window and yelled: 'Pray, good people, be civil – I am the *Protestant* whore!'

Described by Bishop Burnet as 'the most indiscreet and the wildest creature that ever was in a court', Nell remained friendly with the King until his death.

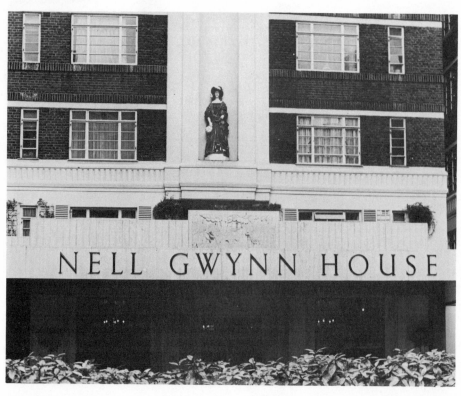

NELL GWYNN HOUSE

RADCLYFFE HALL

1880–1943
Buried: Highgate
Cemetery (West), Swains
Lane, N6

Christened Marguerite, later
known to her friends as John,
Radclyffe Hall moved away from
her mother's home when she was
twenty-one and lived with her

It is the view of this court that this is
a most dangerous and corrupting
book . . . that it is a disgusting
book, that it is an obscene book, a
book which is prejudicial to the
morals of the community. (Sir
Robert Wallace, giving the decision
of the appeal court, December
1928)

grandmother in Kensington.

A lesbian, she dressed very
elegantly in masculine style and
had several affairs with women but
only two serious relationships. The
first was with Mabel Batten, who
encouraged her to write; the
second was with Una Troubridge.
Radclyffe Hall's best-known book,
The Well of Loneliness, was a plea
for the better understanding and
acceptance of lesbianism. It was
published by Jonathan Cape in
1928 and James Douglas, editor of
The Sunday Express at the time,
wrote an article fiercely attacking
it and calling for its suppression. The
Home Secretary recommended its
withdrawal, and Cape agreed, but
the moulds were sent to Paris,
where it was re-printed and copies
smuggled into England. These
were seized and an order against
the book was applied for under the
Obscene Publications Act by the
Director of Public Prosecutions.

Proceedings began at Bow Street
Magistrates Court before the Chief
Magistrate, Sir Chartres Biron. He
declared the book an obscene libel
and ordered that the seized copies
should be destroyed. An appeal
was later dismissed.

Radclyffe Hall died in London.
She was buried in Highgate
Cemetery (West) in the catacomb
of her first lover, Mabel Batten. A
plaque on the side of the crumbling
entrance reads:

> Radclyffe Hall
> 1943
> . . . And, if God choose
> I shall but love thee better
> after death.
> UNA

EMMA, LADY HAMILTON

1765–1815
(née Lyon)
Portrait: Tate Gallery,
Millbank, SW1

The interior of Merton
Church, SW19 where
Nelson is said to have
placed a gold ring on
Emma Hamilton's finger

My dearest Beloved . . . To say that
I think of you by day, night, and all
day, and all night, but too faintly
expresses my feelings of love and
affection towards you.

Whatever has been said – and a
great deal has been said – about
Emma Hamilton, nothing can alter
the fact that she inspired a
romantic, all-consuming passion in
the man who was to become the
archetypal British hero, Horatio,
Lord Nelson.

Emma lived with Sir William
Hamilton in Naples for several
years before she married him in St
Marylebone Church, London, in
1791. She was twenty-six, he was
sixty-one. They returned to Naples
and it was there, two years later,
that she and Nelson met for the
first time and they began a
passionate affair. Emma became
pregnant and gave birth to a
daughter named Horatia [see
Horatia Ward]. Nelson's marriage
finally fell apart, and by October

1807 the Hamiltons and Nelson
were living together at Merton, in
Surrey. In 1803 Sir William died in
Emma's arms and holding
Nelson's hand.

Emma began to drink heavily
and to spend extravagantly. In
August 1805 she was with Nelson
at Merton, in September he
boarded the *Victory* at Plymouth,
on October 21 he was killed at the
Battle of Trafalgar. From then on
Emma's life became a pathetic
record of debt, drink and
bitterness. In 1812, she fled to
France, taking her daughter
Horatia with her. She died at
Calais and was buried in a
cemetery just outside the town.
The captains and masters of
English ships in Calais harbour are
said to have come ashore to attend
her burial:

> Ever, for ever I am yours, only
> yours, even beyond this world . . .
> For ever, for ever, your own
> Nelson.

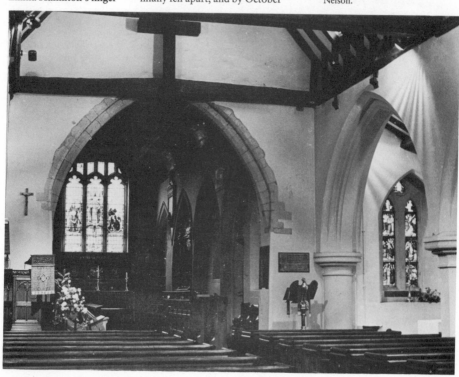

KATE HAMILTON

fl. 1850
Leicester Square WC2
(Kate's Club no longer exists!)

Samuel Beeton's satirical poem *The Siliad* (1873), describing the 'hot-spots' of London in the 1800s, included Kate's 'club' and also Kate:

> O, buxom woman! handsome in thy day,
> Whose gay career th'police courts cannot stay.

The club was in fact a brothel and Kate one of the queens of London night-life. Her career began, apparently, with her participation in 'poses plastiques', the Victorian version of strip-tease.

The luxurious brothel became the resort of disreputable society: to enter her domain one had to be 'known', or sponsored. Inside, a very large Kate, covered with jewels, sat on a velvet throne sipping champagne; at the other end of the room was the bar. Surrounded by pretty girls, she gave orders, supervised the proceedings and occasionally shook with contented laughter.

Kate's origins and details about the end of her life are so far unknown.

ALICE HARGREAVES

1852–1934
(née Liddell)
Born: Dean's Yard,
Westminster Abbey, SW1

A large rose-tree stood near the entrance of the garden: the roses growing on it were white, but there were three gardeners at it, busily painting them red. Alice thought this a very curious thing, and she went nearer to watch them.

The real 'Alice in Wonderland' was born at 19 Dean's Yard, Westminster. Her father, the headmaster of Westminster School, became Dean of Christ Church, Oxford, in 1855 and the following year his family joined him. It was at Oxford that Charles Lutwidge Dodgson ('Lewis Carroll') became a regular visitor, took photographs of Alice and her sisters and began a story while boating on the river:

Alice was beginning to get very tired of sitting by her sister on the bank, and of having nothing to do . . .

Later, something in the relationship went wrong. Nobody seems to know what happened . . . Charles Dodgson's diary appears to have been tampered with and he was no longer welcomed by the Liddell family.

Alice later married and became Alice Hargreaves. She lived in Hampshire, died in Westerham, Kent, and was cremated at Golders Green. (Her ashes were placed in the Hargreaves grave at Lyndhurst.)

So Alice got up and ran off, thinking while she ran, as well she might, what a wonderful dream it had been.

SARAH HECKFORD

1839–1903
(née Goff)
Queen Elizabeth Hospital for Children, Hackney Road, E2

In 1866 Sarah Goff, a wealthy young woman, was working as a volunteer at the Wapping Fever Hospital in London during the cholera epidemic. She met Dr Nathaniel Heckford there and married him the following year. With the help of Sarah's money they founded the East London Hospital for Children and Dispensary for Women, which later led to a hospital at Shadwell, and finally to the present Queen Elizabeth Hospital for Children in Hackney Road.

In 1871 Dr Heckford died and Sarah, after a journey to India, left England for South Africa. There,

after working as a governess, she bought some land, farmed it for a while and then became a 'trader', travelling with wagons and selling her goods through the countryside. She continued this unusual occupation throughout the Boer War.

Although Sarah returned to England for some years, publishing *A Lady Trader in the Transvaal* (1882), a novel called *Excelsior*, and also opening a co-operative store in Woolwich, she eventually decided to go back to South Africa. She died there and was buried in Pretoria.

BARBARA HEPWORTH

1903–1975
Sculpture: outside John
Lewis, Oxford Street, W1

. . . My studio was a jumble of
children, rocks, sculptures, trees,
importunate flowers and washing.

One of the first, also one of the
best, British abstract sculptors,
Barbara Hepworth was born in
Yorkshire and trained in Leeds.
Living in London after her second
marriage (to Ben Nicholson) she
gave birth to triplets:

> On October 3rd Ben and I went to
> the cinema in Belsize Park . . . Ben
> had complained a little bit that I

seemed withdrawn and
concentrated over my pregnancy.
But suddenly I said, 'Oh dear', and
in next to no time I saw three small
children at the foot of my bed –
looking pretty determined and
fairly belligerent.

From 1939 she settled in St Ives,
Cornwall, where the Barbara
Hepworth Museum, studios and
garden were handed over to the
nation in 1980 (she died tragically
in a fire at her home). Examples of
her work are in the Tate Gallery.

Barbara Hepworth's
winged figure (1963) on
the side of John Lewis,
Oxford Street, W1

CAROLINE HERSCHEL

1750–1848
Royal Astronomical Society, Burlington House, Piccadilly, W1

William Herschel discovered the planet Uranus in 1781; his son, John Frederick, also became an astronomer and is buried in Westminster Abbey. Caroline, William's sister and John's aunt, was born in Hanover, Germany, but spent fifty years of her life in England. Joining her brother at Bath in 1772, she became his housekeeper, learned English, shared his enthusiasm for music, studied mathematics and gradually became his chief assistant astronomer. They moved to Windsor and then to Slough, close enough to London for Caroline to visit regularly and to keep in touch with the Royal Astronomical Society, as she was beginning to make her own discoveries. In 1788 she wrote to the Astronomer Royal:

Dear Sir,
Last night, December 21st at 7h 45′, I discovered a comet, a little more than one degree south – preceding β Lyrae. This morning, between five and six, I saw it again, when it appeared to have moved about a quarter of a degree towards δ of the same constellation. I beg the favour of you to take it under your protection . . .

A salary of fifty pounds a year was settled on her, as William's assistant, by the King, and in 1798 her *Index to Flamsteed's Observations of the Fixed Stars* was presented and published by the Royal Society. After her brother's death in 1822 she returned to Hanover. The Royal Astronomical Society voted her a gold medal for her work and later made her an Honorary Member.

OCTAVIA HILL

1838–1912
First housing scheme near Nottingham Place, W1

What we care most to leave those who follow us is not a tangible thing, however great; not any memory, however good; but the quick eye to see, the true soul to measure, the large hope to grasp the mighty issues of the new and better days to come – greater ideals, greater hope, and patience to realise both.

Octavia Hill was a fighter who devoted all her life to social reform. In her teens, while living in London, she was put in charge of a co-operative workshop, where small girls from the Ragged Schools were trained to make toys. Later she became interested and involved in housing reform and ran a housing scheme, initially financed by her friend John Ruskin, the art critic. She collected the rents herself, soon became an authority on the management of tenement houses and her methods began to spread across the country. Her attempts to save existing open spaces in London led to the formation of the Open Spaces Committee of the Kyrle Society. She also worked with the Commons Preservation Society but her greatest achievement in this field was when, in 1895, with Canon Rawnsley and Sir Robert Hunter, she founded the National Trust: 'We have got our first piece of property; I wonder whether it will be the last.'

Octavia Hill's work on housing continued to expand and house-management schemes based on her ideas sprang up abroad. She gave evidence before the Commission on Old Age Pensions, the Commission on Housing and, at almost seventy, began work on the Poor Law Commission. She once said:

When I am gone, I hope my friends will not try to carry out any special system or to follow blindly in the track which I have trodden. New circumstances require various efforts; and it is the spirit, not the dead form, that should be perpetuated.

ADELINE HORSEY DE HORSEY

1824–1915
(Countess of Cardigan
and de Lancastre)
Lived: Upper Grosvenor
Street, W1

Adeline's maiden name –
combined with the information
that she was an excellent
horsewoman – usually provokes
either hilarity or disbelief.
Nevertheless, 'de Horsey' she
remained until she became Lady
Cardigan, a transition that took
some time, as her husband-to-be,
hero of the charge of the Light
Brigade, was already married when
she first met him: 'Among those
who came to our house at 8 Upper
Grosvenor Street, the Earl of
Cardigan was my father's
particular friend . . .'

More than sixty years later she
recalled an incident from those
early days. Her father refused
permission for her to attend the
theatre one evening. He had, he
said, to dine with a colleague and it
would be immoral for her to go
alone. Waiting until he left the
house, Adeline slipped out, sending
a message to Lord Cardigan to
meet her at the theatre. He arrived,
very agitated, and insisted that she
leave at once. Asked why, he
replied:

> Miss de Horsey, your father and
> General Cavendish are in the box
> opposite – with their mistresses! It
> will never do for you to be seen. Do,
> I implore you, permit me to escort
> you home.

Seized with 'an uncontrollable
desire to laugh', Adeline stayed to
watch the play, concealed behind

the curtains of her box. She arrived
home late and her father opened
the door. '"Adeline," said papa in
an awful voice, "Explain yourself.
Where have you been?"' Adeline
told him!

Her relationship with Lord
Cardigan finally caused such a
scandal that she quarrelled with
her father, left home and moved
into a house off Park Lane. Cut by
society she and Cardigan coolly
rode together in the Park almost
every day. Then his wife died and
he was able to propose with the
immortal words: 'My dearest,
she's dead . . . Let's get married at
once.'

They spent much of their
married life at Deene Park,
Northamptonshire and in 1868
Cardigan died there. He left
everything to Adeline. She
hesitated over a proposal from
Disraeli: 'He had, however, one
drawback so far as I was
concerned, and that was his breath
– the ill odour of politics perhaps!'
– and in 1873 she married the
Count de Lancastre.

Adeline published her
Recollections in 1909 and was
over ninety when she died. She is
buried in St Peter's Church, Deene.

DAME FANNY LUCY HOUSTON

1857–1936
(née Radmall)
Buried: St Marylebone
Cemetery, East Finchley,
N2

One of the first Dames of the
British Empire, Lucy Radmall was
born in Lambeth and started a
career on the stage. Married three
times, she was always interested in
women's welfare and founded the
first rest home for exhausted
nurses during the First World War.

Her third husband, Sir R. P.
Houston, died in 1926, leaving her
a fortune of staggering
proportions. Deeply patriotic (she
once painted the rooms of her
house red, white and blue), her
greatest gesture was a contribution
of £100,000 to the Schneider

Trophy aviation contest in 1931,
when the government had refused
financial assistance. Flight-
Lieutenant Stainforth won, flying a
Supermarine Rolls-Royce S6, thus
ensuring the development of
Britain's Spitfires and Hurricanes
used during the Second World
War.

Though she was considered
autocratic and eccentric, many
people nevertheless gratefully
accepted her money. She died in
Hampstead.

MARY ANN HUGHES

1770–1853
Amen Corner, EC4

Mary Ann was born in Uffington and married the local vicar. When he became Canon Residentiary of St Paul's Cathedral they moved to London, and lived in Amen Corner; it was then she met Richard Barham, a minor canon of the cathedral. She encouraged him to write poetry and her rich fund of folklore, ballads and ghost stories inspired his *Ingoldsby Legends*. In the copy he presented to her he wrote:

> To Mrs Hughes who *made* me do'em,
> Quod placeo est – si placeo – tuum.
> (Whatever pleases – if it pleases – is yours.)

She also met Walter Scott, Dickens and Harrison Ainsworth (who wrote her into his novel *Old St Paul's* as 'Mrs Compton'.) After her husband's death she moved to Kingston Lisle, near Uffington. Her grandson, Thomas Hughes, wrote *Tom Brown's Schooldays*.

LUCY HUTCH-INSON

1620–?
(née Apsley)
Born: Tower of London, EC3

It was on the 29th day of January
... that in the Tower of London ...
I was, about four of the clock in the
morning, brought forth to behold
the ensuing light ...

Daughter of the Lieutenant of the
Tower, Lucy Apsley proved to be a
precocious little girl, reading
perfectly by the time she was four
years old and progressing easily to
the classics:

> My father would have me learn
> Latin, and I was so apt that I
> outstripped my brothers who were
> at school, although my father's
> chaplain, that was my tutor, was a
> pitiful dull fellow.

In 1638 she married Colonel
Hutchinson, a member of the first
two councils of state in the
Commonwealth. She bore his
children, lived through the siege of
Nottingham with him when he was
Governor of Nottingham Castle,
visited him daily during his
imprisonment in Sandown Castle

at the Restoration, and, after his
death in prison, wrote his
memoirs:

> In no work that has come down the
> stream of time will be found such a
> vivid and distinct picture of the
> antagonism and mortal strife of the
> seventeenth century, as in the
> Memoir of the Governor of
> Nottingham Castle. (Introduction
> to Memoirs, published 1848)

Although several historians,
among them Catherine Macaulay
(q.v.), had requested the release of
the original manuscript held by the
Hutchinson family it was not
published until the nineteenth
century. Perhaps the worst
disappointment today is that the
memoirs of her husband were
intact, but most of Lucy's lively
account of herself had been
destroyed. Pages had been torn out
and her own life reduced to a
tantalising fragment.

AGNES IBBETSON

1757–1823
(née Thomson)
No address traced so far

Agnes Ibbetson was born in
London but died at Exmouth.
Very little is known about her
except that she studied geology,
mineralogy and astronomy. Her
main subject, however, was botany
and she became a vegetable
physiologist:

> In this her favourite pursuit, she will
> long be known to the world, as her
> observations are most honorably
> recorded, not only in Nicholson's

and other scientific Journals, but
their substance is also transferred
and copied into the Edinburgh and
other Natural Encyclopedias, and
already have received testimonies of
high respect and appreciation ...
(The Gentleman's Magazine, 1823)

According to the Dictionary of
National Biography, Agnes
contributed more than fifty papers
on the microscopic structure and
physiology of plants.

ANNA JAMESON

1794–1860
(née Murphy)
Buried: Kensal Green
Cemetery, NW10

> All that it hoped
> My heart believed
> And when most loving
> Was most deceived ...
>
> I ask no pity
> I hope no cure –
> The heart, tho' broken,
> Can live, and endure.

Anna Jameson, in spite of a
notoriously unhappy marriage,
endured. She began a solid literary
career with Diary of an Ennuyée,
progressed through volumes such
as The Loves of the Poets and
Characteristics of Women (essays
on Shakespeare's female
characters).

She occupied whatever time was
left over by studying and writing
about various aspects of art and
was putting the finishing touches
to Sacred and Legendary Art just
before her death.

> I make no plaint
> I breathe no sigh
> My lips can smile
> And mine eyes are dry.

REBECCA JARRETT

1846–1928
Buried: Abney Park
Cemetery, Stoke
Newington, N16

In the archives of the Salvation Army Headquarters in London lies the manuscript of a short autobiography by Rebecca Jarrett. With devastating honesty (but no punctuation), it recounts incidents in her life starting with her introduction to the dubious delights of Cremorne Gardens:

> I was only 12 years of age My mother was a bit proud of me I was inclined to be tall very fair hair . . . I remember [I] had round my neck a string of great blue beads she kept me clean that was my attraction I never walk the streets she was very particular and kept me very clean so Cremorne Gardens was my ruin before I was 13 . . . she was a good mother it was my Father doing He left her several times and lived with other women my poor Mother was left with 8 children.

Rebecca became a prostitute and an alcoholic. Rescued by the Salvation Army and rehabilitated by Josephine Butler (q.v.) at Winchester, she was eventually allowed to run a small home for 'fallen women' there. Then, in 1885, W. T. Stead, journalist and editor of the *Pall Mall Gazette*, decided to expose the scandal of child prostitution. He needed expert help to prove his case and Rebecca was chosen as a suitable –

if reluctant – agent. She 'bought' a thirteen-year-old girl, Eliza Armstrong, under false pretences from her mother. The child was secretly examined, spirited away, hidden in France and looked after there by the Salvation Army. Stead then wrote a series of articles called 'The Maiden Tribute of Modern Babylon', a superbly successful piece of sensational journalism.

In October 1885 Rebecca Jarrett, W. T. Stead, Bramwell Booth (son of the founder of the Salvation Army) and 'others' were tried at the Old Bailey, accused of unlawfully taking Eliza out of the possession of her parents. Stead was imprisoned for three months, Rebecca for six, but in consequence of their action, a bill was hurried through Parliament raising the age of consent to sixteen for girls.

Rebecca Jarrett, after her release from Millbank Prison, remained with the Salvation Army for the rest of her life.

GERTRUDE JEKYLL

1843–1932
Grafton Street, W1

Although she was born in London, Gertrude Jekyll's family moved to Surrey when she was five and it was there that she began to develop her love and understanding of the English countryside. A copy of the Rev. C. A. John's *Flowers of the Field*, given to her at this time, remained one of her most precious possessions.

When she was eighteen she enrolled at the Kensington School of Art in London and studied there for two years. She then travelled extensively abroad and returned to expand her ability in the field of art and crafts. In 1870, the Duke of Westminster asked her to advise on the furnishings at Eaton Hall. She designed six silk-embroidered

panels for the drawing room there.

In 1867 she moved, with her mother, to Munstead House near Godalming, in Surrey, and her interest in gardens, which had never faded, began to increase. The foundations of her own garden at Munstead were laid out, she became friendly with William Robinson, contributing articles to his magazine *The Garden* and, in 1881, was asked to judge at the Botanic Show, forerunner of the Chelsea Flower Show. She also took up photography and, in 1889, met the young architect Edwin Lutyens for the first time.

Two years later, an eye specialist diagnosed severe myopia and Gertrude had to give up most of her 'fine work'. Fortunately she was able to continue gardening. Her garden at Munstead began to attract great interest and, in 1897, she received the Victoria Medal of Honour from the Royal Horticultural Society.

Meanwhile her friendship with Edwin Lutyens flourished and he designed a new home, Munstead Wood for her, close to the old one. From this sprang their well-known and sensitive collaboration, working together on the designs of a 'Lutyens house' with a 'Jekyll garden'. Gertrude also continued to write and the first of her many

books, *Wood and Garden*, was published in 1899.

When she was in her seventies, William Nicholson painted her portrait, which now hangs in the National Portrait Gallery in London. She was buried in St John the Baptist church at Busbridge and Edwin Lutyens designed the memorial. The inscription reads:

> Artist
> Gardener
> Craftswoman

GWEN JOHN

1876–1939
Trained: Slade School of Fine Art, Gower Street, WC1

Few on meeting this retiring person in black, with her tiny hands and feet, a soft, almost inaudible voice, and delicate Pembrokeshire accent, would have guessed that here was the greatest woman artist of her age, or, as I think, of any other.
(*Finishing Touches*, Augustus John)

Gwendolen Mary John was born in Haverfordwest, Wales. After her mother's death the family moved to Tenby, a seaside resort close by. Gwen and her brother Augustus both sketched from an early age and, in 1894, Augustus went to the Slade School of Art in London. She followed him there in 1895 and soon won a certificate for figure drawing and later a prize for figure composition. Three years later she moved to Paris and, although she returned to London for a brief period, spent most of the rest of her life in France.

Gwen John, shy, intense, proud, independent and uncompromising, produced her paintings slowly and painfully, supporting herself by working as an artist's model. She

posed for Rodin, the sculptor and fell passionately in love with him. In 1913 she was converted to the Catholic faith and became friendly with the nuns at a convent in the suburb of Meudon. Later she bought herself a home there, described by Augustus as 'a mere shed', where she lived with her beloved cats. John Quinn, an American collector, paid her an allowance for many years and so acquired much of her work.

One day in 1939 she took a train to Dieppe and died at the Hospice de Dieppe.

> You are free only when you have left all.
> Leave everybody and let them leave you.
> Then only will you be without fear.
> (Gwen John)

AMY JOHNSON

1903–1941
(**Mrs Mollison**)
Married: St George's Church, St George Street, W1

Born and educated in Hull, Yorkshire, Amy Johnson moved to London where she worked as a secretary. In 1928 she joined the London Aeroplane Club and soon gained her pilot's and engineer's licences.

She became the first woman to fly solo from England to Australia in 1930 and continued to pioneer other routes and set other records.

In 1941, while ferrying an Airspeed Oxford for Air Transport, she disappeared over the Thames Estuary. She may have run out of fuel, baled out and drowned.

DOROTHY JORDAN

1761–1816
(née Bland)
Plaque: 30 Cadogan
Place, SW1

An illegitimate child, Dorothy was born in London and put on the stage at an early age by her mother. They later moved to Dublin and joined the theatre there, in Smock Alley, but Dorothy was seduced by the manager and became pregnant. She and her mother returned hurriedly to England where Dorothy toured with Tate Wilkinson's company. In 1785 she appeared in London in Wycherley's *The Country Girl* in which she was a great success.

She lived with Sir Richard Ford and presented him with three children, but in 1790 people began to notice that one of George III's sons, William, Duke of Clarence, was taking a great interest in her. She became his mistress and lived with him for over twenty years, bearing him ten children. They were very happy and domesticated, although always short of money and, to supplement the housekeeping, Dorothy continued to work in the theatre. In 1797 they moved into Bushy House, in Bushy Park near Hampton Court.

Life continued as usual until, in 1811, the King became gravely ill and William decided to look for a suitable consort. The news that their relationship was at an end reached Dorothy while she was on tour; they met at Maidenhead to say goodbye. Her behaviour was impeccable and she received a great deal of public sympathy. A settlement was reached, she moved from Bushy House to Cadogan Place and returned to the stage.

Unfortunately her favourite son-in-law then got badly into debt and, convinced that she was liable, she fled to France to avoid arrest in 1815. Expecting some help and reassurance, she seems to have received none. Dorothy Jordan then moved to St Cloud, where her health rapidly deteriorated and where she died.

Her epitaph (written later by John Genest, the theatrical historian) ended:

> Mementote, lugete – Remember . . . and weep for her

ANGELICA KAUFFMANN

1741–1807
Royal Academy of Art,
Piccadilly, W1

A Swiss artist, Angelica Kauffmann lived in London from 1766. She became a founder member of the Royal Academy and frequently exhibited there. Some of her work can still be seen on the ceiling of the entrance hall.

Her unfortunate marriage to a bogus 'Count' was dissolved, and she was believed to have had an affair with Sir Joshua Reynolds. In 1781 she married a Venetian painter, Antonio Zucchi and left England. She died in Rome.

In 1875 Anne Thackeray Ritchie (q.v.) published *Miss Angel*, a novel based on the artist's life. In it, she describes a portrait of Angelica:

> Yesterday, at Mr Colnaghi's, I saw a print lying on the table, the engraving of one of Sir Joshua's portraits. It was the picture of a lady some five or six and twenty years of age. The face is peculiar, sprightly, tender, a little obstinate. The eyes are very charming and intelligent. The features are broadly marked; there is something at once homely and dignified in their expression.

FANNY (FRANCES) KEMBLE

1809–1893
(Mrs Butler)
Buried: Kensal Green
Cemetery, NW10

Being a Kemble was almost synonymous with being an actress, so when Fanny first appeared at Covent Garden as Juliet in 1829 – and was a great success – no one was at all surprised. Some eyebrows *were* raised a few years later, when it became known that, while touring America, she had married Pierce Butler, settled there

. . . and given up the theatre.

In 1835 she published *Journal of a Residence in America* and gave birth to a daughter. All should have been well, but Fanny could not conform to the restricted life she was expected to lead; her husband's family disapproved of her and her marriage was showing signs of strain. Bored, restless and

Fanny Kemble contd.

missing England, she threw herself into an absorbing interest, the abolition of slavery – a subject hardly likely to improve matters, as her in-laws owned land, and slaves, in Georgia!

After the birth of a second daughter Fanny visited the family estates, where she not only campaigned enthusiastically, particularly against the slavery of women, but also attempted to improve conditions for them. At this point, their marriage almost in ruins, Pierce took her on a visit to England, but it was too late . . . total breakdown and a separation came on their return to America.

In 1845, forbidden to see her daughters, Fanny sailed for England. She went back to America only for the divorce proceedings and also when her

daughters came of age and she was, at last, allowed to visit them.

Fanny Kemble suffered greatly. As Anne Thackeray Ritchie (q.v.) later wrote of her:

. . . when strong feeling, vivid realisations, passionate love of truth and justice, uncompromising faith exist, then experience becomes hard indeed.

However, when she was nearly seventy she published her *Recollections of a Girlhood*, memoirs that brim over with high spirits, a sense of fun and an unquenchable love of life:

I have come to the garrulous time of life – to the remembering days, which only by a little precede the forgetting ones.

KATHLEEN, LADY KENNET
1878–1947
(Lady Scott)
(née Bruce)
Her statue of Captain Scott: Waterloo Place, SW1;
Bust of Lord Northcliff: outside St Dunstan's-in-the-West, Fleet Street, EC4

Mr Asquith came and sat in the studio till eight. He said I had the best brain of any woman he had ever met. I said, 'Say that again'; and he said it again. (from Lady Kennet's *Self-Portrait of an Artist*)

In 1899 Kathleen Bruce became a student at the Slade School of Art in London. She then studied sculpture at Colarossi's Studios in Paris and, in 1906, returned to live and work in London. Two years later she married Captain R. F. Scott in the chapel at Hampton Court Palace, and in 1909 gave birth to a son, Peter (the famous naturalist, Peter Scott).

When Captain Scott went to join his ship in Australia, prepared for the second Antarctic expedition, Kathleen accompanied him and saw him off as the ship left New Zealand in November 1910. She went back to London, where she lived in Buckingham Palace Road. The following year she wrote in her diary:

One hasn't got one's husband in the body, but one has got him so very firmly in the spirit that it spoils everything. One can't think of loving anybody else, and yet one's whole being is crying out, 'You are young, you are healthy, go out and

love.' I think decidedly I had better get back to work.

In January 1913 Kathleen Scott left for the United States on her way to meet her husband in New Zealand. On 5 February she joined her ship at San Francisco and on the 19 February the Captain showed her the message breaking the news about the expedition: 'Captain Scott and six others perished in blizzard after reaching South Pole January 18.'

Her statue of her husband was unveiled by Mr Balfour in 1915. It stands in Waterloo Place, just north of the Mall. Kathleen married the Liberal MP Hilton Young (later Lord Kennet) in 1922 and a year later gave birth to another son. In 1941 she wrote to her second husband:

Here is what you shall put on my tiny grave-stone. 'Kathleen. No happier woman ever lived.'

Kathleen Kennet's statue of her first husband, Robert Falcon Scott, unveiled in 1915 in Waterloo Place, SW1. In his diary he wrote: 'My dear, what dreams I have had of the future.'

ANNIE KENNEY

1879–1953
(Mrs Taylor)
Lambeth Palace, Lambeth
Palace Road, SE1

Annie was born in Lancashire. Her parents were poor and before she was thirteen she became a 'half-timer' – half the day spent at school, the other half working in a cotton-mill. From the age of fourteen she worked full-time, but a lively mind such as hers could never be content with a humdrum existence, and, influenced by the writings of Robert Blatchford (Socialist writer and philosopher), she was deeply impressed when she heard Christabel Pankhurst speak on Women's Suffrage and Trades Unionism. In 1905 Annie was sentenced to three days' imprisonment for her part in the disruption of a meeting in the Free Trade Hall in Manchester.

She then moved to London, where she soon became one of the leaders of the more militant Women's Social and Political Union, was imprisoned and went on hunger-strike.

A newspaper photograph of the time shows a small, slim, very attractive young woman being led away by two large, unsmiling, male Police Officers. Her face is alight with a wide and mischievous grin. Annie, for all her political and religious idealism, revelled in the more dramatic escapades of the Suffragettes, loved disguises and once avoided capture by hiding in a theatrical hamper labelled 'Marie Lloyd'. She made a well-publicised attempt to involve the Archbishop of Canterbury by lying on the pavement outside Lambeth Palace until she was removed in an ambulance.

After her marriage to James Taylor she lived in Letchworth, Hertfordshire, and quietly faded from the scene.

MARY KINGSLEY

1862–1900
Plaque: 22 Southwood
Lane, Highgate, N6

A plaque in Southwood Lane, Highgate, marks the house where Mary, aged twelve and 'experimenting' with gunpowder in the garden, blew a container of liquid manure all over the family washing. The rest of her life was to prove equally exciting.

When her parents both died in 1892 Mary decided to travel, continuing her father's life-long interests. She left, unaccompanied, on a cargo boat and explored parts of the Congo, studying local customs, collecting specimens and making notes. Her second visit

included a hair-raising journey from the Ogowe to the Rembwe river through the great forest, accompanied by four Africans. On her return she wrote her first book, *Travels in West Africa* (1897), a huge success, partly due to Mary's unique sense of humour. Tongue in cheek, she gives advice:

> When you get into the way, catching a snake in a cleft stick is perfectly simple. Only mind you have the proper kind of stick . . . and keep your attention on the snake's head, that's his business end . . . the tail, whisking and winding round your wrist, does not matter.

Exhausted, she arrives at a European 'station':

> I am in an awful mess – mud-caked skirts, and blood-stained hands and face. Shall I make an exhibition of myself and wash here, or make an exhibition of myself by going unwashed to the unknown German officer in charge . . . ? Naturally I wash here, standing in the river and . . . wading across to the other bank, wring out my skirts: but what is life without a towel?

In 1900, in the Boer War, Mary went to the Cape as a nurse. She died there of enteric fever and was buried at sea, as she had wished.

DAME LAURA KNIGHT

1877–1970
(née Johnson)
Lived: 16 Langford Place,
St John's Wood, NW8

Laura Johnson was born near Nottingham and studied at Nottingham School of Art. She married Harold Knight, who was also an artist, in 1903. They lived in Cornwall for some years, but from 1919 they made London their base, with studios in St John's Wood.

She was a prolific and, during her lifetime, a highly celebrated artist. In 1936 she was elected a Royal Academician and in 1946 was the official artist at the Nuremberg Trials. The subjects that most appealed to her,

however, were those connected with the theatre, the ballet and the circus:

> Dame Laura Knight
> Had unusually keen sight.
> She could spot a circus clown, they say,
> A couple of miles away.
> (E. Clerihew Bentley)

LADY CAROLINE LAMB

1785–1828
Died: Melbourne House, Whitehall, SW1 (now the Scottish Office)

The incredible Lady Caroline . . .
> 'with pleasures too refined to please,
> With too much spirit to be e'er at ease,
> With too much quickness to be ever taught,
> With too much thinking to have common thought'.
> (*Queen Victoria*, Lytton Strachey)

Daughter of the third Earl of Bessborough, Caroline was taken to Italy at the age of three. She remained there for six years, mainly under the supervision of servants. On her return to London she was found to be a rather unusual little girl!

Married to William Lamb, later Lord Melbourne, she became notorious through her wild infatuation for the poet, Lord Byron. Caroline noted in her diary that Byron was . . . 'mad, bad and

dangerous to know', and when the affair was over, one of her novels, *Glenarron*, published anonymously in 1816, contained a thinly disguised caricature of him.

Always excitable to the point of instability, it was said that she became 'mentally deranged' after accidentally meeting Byron's funeral procession. Caroline died four years later and was buried in (Old) Hatfield Church.

MARY LAMB

1764–1847
Born: Crown Office Row, Temple, EC4 [Plaque to Charles Lamb]

Mary was one of seven children, and the sister of Charles Lamb. Mrs Gilchrist, an early biographer, described her as: '. . . a shy, sensitive, nervous, affectionate child who early showed signs of a liability to brain disorder.' It took many years before those early signs erupted into tragedy. In 1795, their father having been pensioned off, the family moved to Queen Street, Holborn. Charles and Mary took on most of the responsibility of caring for their ageing parents.

Mary helped to supplement the meagre family income by taking in millinery work. Quite soon she had to hire an apprentice to help her and she was already working too hard when another brother became ill and had to be nursed.

There are slightly differing versions as to what happened when Mary suddenly broke under the strain. One is that she attacked the apprentice with a knife, that her mother tried to intervene and was fatally stabbed instead. Mary spent some time in an asylum in Islington where she gradually recovered. Charles then found her rooms in Hackney and visited her on Sundays and holidays, but she was soon back in the asylum.

In 1799 their father died and Mary went home. From then on Charles cared for her with devotion and understanding. She began to write, and shared with her brother the authorship of their *Tales from Shakespeare* (1807) and, later, *Mrs Leicester's School*.

Mary Lamb fought her disability, although she spent regular periods in the asylum, but gradually slipped into a state of isolation. She survived Charles by thirteen years and is buried with him in Edmonton churchyard.

JESSICA LANDSEER

1807–1880
Lived: St John's Wood Road, NW8

Her unselfishness and large-heartedness struck me at times as something heroic . . . The skill and tact with which she managed her brother's house never failed.
(G. D. Leslie)

Jessica was born in London, a daughter of John Landseer the engraver and his wife Jane. She painted miniatures, landscapes, learned to etch and had ten of her pictures exhibited at the Royal Academy. For almost thirty years she was the devoted housekeeper and companion of her famous brother, the artist Sir Edwin Landseer, at his home in St John's Wood. As Sir Edwin suffered from depression, alcoholism and later severe mental disturbance, this can have been no easy task. She was with him when he died in 1873. She died at Folkestone seven years later.

LILLIE (EMILIE) LANGTRY

1853–1929
(née Le Breton)
Plaque: The Cadogan Hotel, Pont Street, SW1

Lillie was the daughter of William le Breton, the Dean of Jersey and Rector of St Saviour's church there. In 1874 she married Edward Langtry, a wealthy ship-owner's son, and three years later they moved to London. There she proceeded to stun artists, writers and society with her beauty and became a cult figure. Her husband fell by the wayside.

For a while she was the mistress of the Prince of Wales (later Edward VII) and it was this relationship that initially packed the theatres when she later became a professional actress. In 1882 she arrived in America where she spent most of the next five years, appearing in various productions, attracting enormous publicity and the subject of endless gossip. She became an exceptionally wealthy woman.

From 1892 to 1897 she lived at 21 Pont Street, London (now the Cadogan Hotel), and two years later married Hugo de Bathe. She was still working in her sixties, but in 1919 Lillie Langtry retired to Monaco, living in a house overlooking the Riviera and aptly named Villa Le Lys. In 1925 she published her autobiography *The Days I Knew*. It gave little away.

She died in France but was buried, at her request, in the churchyard of St Saviour's, Jersey.

Oh, never, never, never since we joined the human race
Saw we so exquisitely fair a face.
(W. S. Gilbert)

VIVIEN LEIGH

1913–1967
(née Hartley)
Memorial Plaque: St
Paul's Church, Covent
Garden, WC2

In 1932, Vivien Hartley enrolled at the Royal Academy of Dramatic Art in London and the same year married Herbert Leigh Holman, a barrister. In 1933 she gave birth to a daughter. Although Vivien then worked in several films, it was not until she appeared in a play called *The Mask of Virtue* at the Ambassadors Theatre that she attracted the attention of Alexander Korda, who offered her a part in his film *Fire Over England*. She played opposite Laurence Olivier, they fell in love and soon afterwards she left her husband.

When Laurence Olivier went to Hollywood in 1938 to star in *Wuthering Heights* Vivien followed him, determined to try for the coveted role of Scarlett O'Hara in the film *Gone With The Wind*. After a long, much-publicised search, the producer, David Selznick, had failed to find the ideal Scarlett. When he met Vivien he gave her a screen-test and promptly offered her the part. In 1939 she won an Oscar for her performance. In 1940 she married Laurence Olivier.

Vivien Leigh made nineteen films altogether, and won a second Oscar, in 1951, for her acting as Blanche DuBois in the film of *A Streetcar Named Desire*. She also worked consistently in the theatre, in parts ranging from the title-role in Anouilh's *Antigone* and Lulu in the farce *Look After Lulu*, to both Shakespeare's and Shaw's *Cleopatra*. Exceptionally beautiful, and also exceptionally highly-strung, she continually overworked, driving herself from one goal to another as if competing in some desperate race. During the filming of *Elephant Walk* in 1953 she collapsed in Hollywood and was flown back to London. She was working again within months.

In 1960 she and Olivier were divorced. Vivien bought Tickerage Mill, a house in the country outside London. The last film she made was Stanley Kramer's *Ship of Fools*, for which she won the French 'Etoile Crystal' award. She died of tuberculosis at Tickerage and her ashes were scattered on the lake there. Her memorial plaque in St Paul's, Covent Garden ends with a quotation from Shakespeare's *Antony and Cleopatra*:

> Now boast thee, death,
> In thy possession lies
> A lass unparallel'd.

CAROLINE LEJEUNE

1897–1973
(Mrs Thompson)
Observer, 8 St Andrew's
Hill, EC4

Miss Lejeune was one of the first critics to treat with equal seriousness and write with equal perception about all kinds of films. For her the important thing was, and is, not to what school a film belonged but whether it was good of its kind. (Sir Michael Balcon)

Caroline Lejeune was born in Manchester and graduated at Manchester University. She became film critic for the *Manchester Guardian* in 1922, married the journalist Roffe Thompson and joined the *Observer* newspaper. She remained film critic for the *Observer* until her retirement in 1960.

As 'C. A. Lejeune', she delighted her readers by occasionally writing some of the shortest and funniest reviews on record. Of the film *Charley's Aunt*, starring Jack Benny, she merely said:

> Can you think of any
> Reason why Jack Benny
> Should play Charley's Aunt?
> I can't.

ROSA LEWIS

1867–1952
(née Ovenden)
The Cavendish Hotel
(rebuilt), Jermyn Street,
SW1

English women *can* be the best
cooks in the world, says Mrs Rosa
Lewis . . . (*The Sketch*, June 1914)

Rosa, the daughter of an
undertaker, was born in Leyton,
now a suburb of London. After
working for a while as a domestic
servant, she became under-
kitchenmaid in the household of
the Comte de Paris at Sheen House
in Mortlake, and learnt the art of
cookery. Five years later she was
Lady Randolph Churchill's cook,
after which there was no looking
back; Rosa had become 'known'
and was much in demand.

In 1893 she married Excelsior
Lewis, Sir Andrew Clarke's butler.
This seems to have been an
'arranged' marriage and their
house, 55 Eaton Terrace, was
apparently used as a 'house of
convenience' by, among others, the

Prince of Wales. Rosa began to
build up her own freelance cookery
business. Using a large staff and
showing brilliant administrative
ability she worked successfully for
Lord Ribblesdale, Sir William
Eden and Waldorf Astor.

In 1902 she bought the
Cavendish Hotel in Jermyn Street
and turned it into one of the most
fashionable hotels in London, at
the same time continuing her
freelance catering. During the First
World War, soldiers were billeted
there; after the war it continued to
be a fashionable, if somewhat
disreputable and eccentric hotel.

Rosa Lewis is said to have been
portrayed as 'Lottie Crump' in
Evelyn Waugh's *Vile Bodies*. She
lived through the Second World
War and was buried in Putney Vale
Cemetery.

Rosa Lewis is buried in
Putney Vale Cemetery,
SW15. 'English women
can be the best cooks in
the world'.

ELIZABETH LILLY

d. 1882
Buried: Highgate
Cemetery (West), Swains
Lane, N6

Mrs Lilly, formerly employed by
the Duchess of Sutherland, became
Queen Victoria's 'monthly nurse'
and attended all the royal
confinements from 1840, including
the birth of Prince Leopold (in
1853), when the new and
controversial chloroform was
administered to the Queen.

It was Mrs Lilly who, hearing a

palace door creak one night, and
getting no reply when she called
out, promptly sent for one of the
Queen's pages. The seventeen-
year-old Edmund Jones, who made
a habit of breaking into
Buckingham Palace, was
discovered hiding under a sofa in
the Queen's sitting-room.

MARIE LLOYD

1870–1922
(née Wood)
Plaque: 55 Graham Road,
E8

Born in the East End of London (Hoxton), Marie Lloyd became the greatest star of the British Music Hall. She first appeared on stage at the age of fifteen and her early songs tended to be sweetly romantic: 'The Boy I Love is up in the Gallery', but her own inimitable style soon began to emerge. In 1891 she appeared, with Dan Leno, at Drury Lane in *Humpty Dumpty. The Daily Telegraph* commented:

The sprightliest of heroines, but some of her attitudes need a little toning down and are unsuitable to the medium of Drury Lane, which is bound to maintain a certain dignity, even in its liveliest moments.

Marie Lloyd's act was based on rich low comedy, songs liberally sprinkled with innuendo and double meanings ('She Sits among the Cabbages and Peas') and vivid portraits of women: 'I'm one of the ruins that Cromwell knocked about a bit!' (the 'Cromwell' was a pub). Generous, extravagant and honest, the public adored her, calling her 'our Marie'.

Justifiably upset and insulted by being left out of the Royal Command Performance in 1912, Marie booked the London Pavilion for the same night and packed it to the doors! She married three times and had one daughter but, at last, unhappy in her private life, unwell and under pressure, she began to drink heavily. Her last performance was at the Edmonton Empire; she collapsed after giving her 'Cromwell' song and died a few days later. Thousands lined the funeral route to Hampstead Cemetery where she is buried.

Marie Lloyd's tombstone in Hampstead Cemetery

DAME KATHLEEN LONSDALE

1903–1971
(née Yardley)
University College,
Gower Street, WC1

At the age of sixty-four, Dame Kathleen Lonsdale, Professor of Chemistry at University College, London, for almost twenty years, remarked:

I am unfortunately at the period when, as a research chemist, I am almost good for nothing. In fact, my only chance of achieving further distinction is to become Speaker of the House of Commons, Prime Minister or Pope, careers for which no doubt experience counts more than creative power.

Kathleen Lonsdale, married in

1927 and with three children, became a highly distinguished crystallographer. She was also a Quaker and a pacifist. In 1943 she served a prison sentence for refusing to register for war duties; in 1945 she was one of the first two women ever to become Fellows of the Royal Society. Made a Dame of the British Empire in 1956, she rounded off her career with a flourish when she was elected the first woman President of the British Association eleven years later.

JANE LOUDON
**1807–1858
(née Webb)**
Plaque: 3 Porchester
Terrace, W2

3 Porchester Terrace, just off Bayswater Road, displays a blue plaque reading: 'Here lived John and Jane Loudon . . . Their Horticultural Work Gave New Beauty to London Squares.'

When, in 1830, John Loudon was invited to meet the author of *The Mummy – A Tale of the Twenty-second Century*, he assumed that he would be introduced to a young man. Instead, he found himself talking to an attractive young woman from Birmingham. Eight months later he married her.

Jane became not only his wife but his secretary. She accompanied him on horticultural projects, learned everything he could teach her about gardening and studied Botany. In 1841, an expert in her own right, the first of her gardening books was published.

After thirteen years of marriage she was widowed and faced with the problem of bringing up their daughter, Agnes, on a small pension. Books, such as *The*

Ladies' Country Companion: Or How to Enjoy a Country Life Rationally supplemented her income. Then she was asked to become editor of a new magazine for women, *The Ladies' Companion: At Home and Abroad.* Jane had scarcely had time to establish herself before it was suggested that she become editor in name only. Her refusal prompted a letter requesting her resignation and, in June 1850, she wrote her last editorial – 'A Few Words on the Condition of Woman'. Mild in tone, and mainly a defence of the 'unmarried' woman, it nevertheless stoutly asserted that '. . . woman's position and the estimation in which she is held by man is a true test of the civilisation of a country'.

After this, Jane Loudon retreated from the fray, travelled a little, prepared another book on gardening and died aged fifty-one. She was buried with her husband in Kensal Green Cemetery.

Jane Loudon lived at 3
Porchester Terrace, W2
with her husband

ADA LOVELACE

1815–1852
(née Byron)
Born: 8 St James's Street,
W1 (now replaced by
'Byron House')

But I feel bound to tell you that the power of thinking on these matters which Lady L. has always shown . . . has been something so utterly out of the common way for any beginner, man or woman, that this power must be duly considered by her friends . . . whether they should urge or check her obvious determination to try not only to reach, but to get beyond, the present bounds of knowledge.
(Professor de Morgan to Ada's mother)

So 'utterly out of the common' was Ada Lovelace, Lord Byron's daughter, that she has recently been described as the first 'programmer' and a computer language named after her.

When she met Charles Babbage, very few people understood the theory behind his 'Difference' and 'Analytical' engines, forerunners of the calculator and computer. Ada not only understood and worked with him, but also translated Menabrea's *Notices sur la machine Analytique de Mr Babbage*, adding her own lengthy and lucid notes.

Beautiful and highly strung, she loved horses and music, was happily married to Lord Lovelace and had three children. She died of cancer in her thirties, her last few years clouded by gambling-debts which she had tried to conceal from her husband.

Ada's parents separated not long after her birth in London. She never met her father, Lord Byron, but at her own wish was buried close to him in the church at Hucknall, near Newstead Abbey.

> Is thy face like thy mother's, my fair child,
> Ada! Sole daughter of my house and heart?
> When last I saw thy young blue eyes they smiled,
> And then we parted.
> (Byron, *Childe Harold's Pilgrimage*)

LADY CONSTANCE LYTTON

1869–1923
Bow Street (Police Court),
WC2

A daughter of the first Earl of Lytton, Lady Constance became a militant suffragette. Arrested in 1909 and sentenced at Bow Street Court, in London, she was sent to Holloway Prison where, almost immediately, she was put into the hospital, on the grounds that she had a weak heart. Although her health was not strong, Lady Constance suspected that she had been given preferential treatment on account of her social position.

In 1910 she disguised herself as 'Jane Warton', an ordinary working-class suffragette, and deliberately set out to be arrested. Imprisoned in Walton Gaol, Liverpool, she went on hunger-strike. They did not bother to examine her heart before she was subjected to forcible feeding and, when she was released and her identity revealed, she protested to the Home Office, saying that they had different rules for the rich and the poor. Her charges were, predictably, denied, but Lady Constance had made her point, although her health was probably permanently impaired as a result.

She wrote *Prisons and Prisoners, Some Personal Experiences by Constance Lytton and Jane Warton, Spinster*, and died in London aged fifty-four.

MARY MACARTHUR

1880–1921
(Mrs Anderson)
Lived: Mecklenburgh
Square, WC1

In 1901, John Turner, Trades Unionist, arrived in Ayr, Scotland, hoping to found a branch of the Shop Assistants Union. Mary Macarthur, book-keeper in her father's drapery store, went to listen to him. She intended to write a hostile article for the local newspaper but found herself so convinced by his arguments that shortly afterwards she became the chairman of the newly-formed Ayr branch of the SAU.

Moving to London in 1903, she was persuaded to become Secretary of the Women's Trade Union League; the membership swiftly rose by over twenty per cent. A whirlwind of energy, Mary spoke at meetings, led deputations and helped to found the National Federation of Women Workers.

Her evidence before a Select Committee of the House of Commons inquiring into sweated labour was painstakingly researched and devastating. In 1909 the Government passed the Trade Boards Act, compelling four of the worst offenders to fix minimum rates of pay. When the employers of women chainmakers at Cradley Heath, Staffordshire, attempted to dodge the issue, Mary Macarthur took part in the organisation and funding of the strike.

Later, in 1911, the year of her marriage to Will Anderson, she became passionately involved in the widespread strikes of the women workers of Bermondsey and during the 1914–18 war she fought for equal pay for men and women in munition work.

She was only just forty when she died after an operation.

CATHARINE MACAULAY

1731–1791
(née Sawbridge)

The statue of Catharine Macaulay now stands in the reference library which forms part of the Museum and Art Gallery at Warrington, Lancashire

Born in Kent, Catharine married Dr George Macaulay in 1760 and moved to London, where she became famous after publishing the first volume of her *History of England*. Her fame was largely political, as she was strongly anti-monarchy and wrote as such; the Whigs adored her and made her their heroine.

After six years of marriage, her husband died and she was left to bring up their only daughter. She continued to write (apparently exceptionally slowly), and then moved to Bath under the patronage and protection of Dr Thomas Wilson, the non-resident Rector of St Stephen's Walbrook church in the City of London. He worshipped her, loaded her with gifts and servants, gave parties for her and finally commissioned her statue. This was placed in St Stephen's Church, with the inscription:

You speak of Mrs Macaulay;
She is a Kind of Prodigy!
I revere her abilities:
I cannot bear to hear her Name
    sarcastically
Mentioned.
I would have her taste the exalted
    Pleasure
of universal Applause;
I would have Statues erected to her
    Memory;
and once in every age I could wish
such a Woman to appear,
As a Proof that Genius is not
    confined to Sex;
But at the same Time – you will
    pardon me –
we want no more than
One Mrs Macaulay.

Then, in her forties, Catharine caused an immense scandal by suddenly marrying twenty-one-year-old William Graham, surgeon's mate and brother of a notorious medical 'quack', 'Dr' Graham (see Ann Curtis). Mrs Macaulay was ridiculed and caricatured . . . Dr Wilson hastily removed her statue from his church and cut her out of his life. She seems to have been quite happy, however, with her new husband who, after her death, carried on a long, acrimonious correspondence (in the *Gentleman's Magazine*) with the elder Disraeli as to whether Catharine, whilst engaged in research, had torn pages from manuscripts in the British Museum. They arrived at no definite conclusion.

She was buried at Binfield, near Windsor.

BLANCHE ROOSEVELT MACCHETTA

1858–1898
(Marchesa d'Allegri)
Buried: Brompton
Cemetery, SW7

Born in Virginia, USA, Blanche Roosevelt Tucker travelled to Europe, lived for a while in France, married, and so became the Marchesa d'Allegri. Based in London, she wrote romances, such as *Stage-struck: or She Would Be an Opera-Singer* (1884) and *The Copper Queen* (1886). Her biographies are perhaps more interesting. She wrote a life of Verdi, and her *Life and Reminiscences of Gustave Doré* (1885) has only recently been used as a source-book for another study of that artist.

Only forty when she died at her home in Montagu Street, London, she was buried in the Brompton Cemetery. Below a graceful statue, the inscription ends:

> By her brilliant accomplishments
> And rare graces of mind and person
> She gave distinction
> In the world of literature and art
> To the name of Blanche Roosevelt.

MARGARET MACDONALD

1870–1911
(née Gladstone)
Memorial (and home):
Lincoln's Inn Fields, WC2

There is a charming and informal memorial (by Richard Goulden) to Margaret MacDonald, the wife of Britain's first Labour Prime Minister, in the gardens of Lincoln's Inn Fields in London. A kneeling woman extends her arms tenderly over a lively group of plump and jolly cherubs.

A tribute to Margaret reads:

She was the daughter of John and Margaret Gladstone; She was born

in Kensington in 1870; was married to J-Ramsay MacDonald in 1896 and lived with him at 3 Lincoln's Inn Fields . . . Here her children were born and here she died in 1911. She brought joy to those with whom and for whom she lived and worked. Her heart went out in fellowship to her fellow-women and in love to the children of the people whom she served as a citizen and helped as a sister. She quickened faith and zeal in others by her life and took no rest from doing good.

SARAH MALCOLM

1710?–1733
Buried: St Sepulchre's
Church, EC1 (graveyard
no longer exists)

If Hogarth had not sketched Sarah in her prison cell and then done a painting of her (National Gallery of Scotland, Edinburgh), she would have faded into obscurity. At the time, the crime she was accused of aroused widespread, grisly interest and a great many prints of Hogarth's portrait were sold at sixpence each!

A country girl, born in Durham, Sarah came to London and worked as a cleaning woman at the Temple. In February 1733 one of her employers, Mrs Duncomb, an elderly widow, was found strangled in bed. Her two servants were also dead (one with her

throat cut from ear to ear) and the house had been robbed. Suspected, Sarah was arrested and tried.

Admitting finally that she had helped to plan and carry out the robbery, she denied the murders, blaming her accomplices. As Sarah knew that she would be hanged merely for robbery, she may have been telling the truth. However, although the three people she had named were detained, she alone was found guilty and executed in Fleet Street. Her corpse was displayed at Snow Hill before being buried in the graveyard of St Sepulchre's church.

MARY DE LA RIVIÈRE MANLEY

d. 1724
Buried: St Benet's Church, Upper Thames Street, EC4

Mrs Manley is said to have gone through a form of marriage with her cousin, who later deserted her. She led a riotous existence and wrote to earn a living. Her play *The Lost Lover: Or the Jealous Husband* was performed in 1696. An accomplished political satirist, her *Secret History of Queen Zarah and the Zarazians etc.* was basically an attack on Sarah Churchill (q.v.) and the Whig Party.

She lived finally with a Mr Barber, an Alderman and printer in the City of London, and died at his printing-house on Lambeth Hill. Buried in the church of St Benet (near St Paul's Cathedral), her inscription read:

Here lies the body of
Mrs de la Rivière Manley
Daughter of Sir Roger Manley, Kt.
Who, suitable to her birth and education, was acquainted with several parts of knowledge; and was the most polite writer both in the French and English tongues. This accomplishment, together with a greater natural stock of wit, made her conversation agreeable to all who knew her, and her writings be universally read with pleasure . . .

KATHERINE MANSFIELD

1888–1923
(Murry)
(née Beauchamp)
Plaque: 17 East Heath Road, NW3

From 1917 onwards all her art, like that of Keats or Stephen Crane, was a function of her dying. (Elizabeth Bowen)

Katherine Mansfield died of consumption in her early thirties at Avon, near Fontainebleau, in France.

She was born in Wellington, New Zealand, and sent to school in London for a brief period. In 1908 she returned to London where she made a disastrous and short-lived marriage to George Bowden and also wrote her first book, *In a German Pension* (1909).

Later she met the critic and editor, John Middleton Murry. They were married at Kensington Register Office in 1918 and lived at 17 East Heath Road, Hampstead. It was a turbulent relationship, and Katherine's health was rapidly deteriorating, but she continued to write and, in 1922, published her best-known collection of short stories, *The Garden Party*.

Her work has been described as that of a miniaturist in prose, and her ability to create atmosphere compared to that of Tchekov but she had little time to prove her worth. In an attempt to regain her health she travelled to Switzerland and then became a follower of the mystic/philosopher Gurdjieff. It was at his home, the Prieuré des Basses Loges, on the outskirts of the forest of Fontainebleau, that she collapsed and died of consumption.

In the cemetery at Avon, the inscription on her grave reads:

Katherine Mansfield, wife of John Middleton Murry,
1888–1923
'But I tell you, my lord fool, out of this nettle, danger, we pluck this flower, safety.'

Her *Journal* was published posthumously in 1927.

Katherine Mansfield's house at 17 East Heath Road, Hampstead

MRS (SARAH?) MAPP

(fl. 1736)
(née Wallin)
Seven Dials, WC2

The Cures performed by the Woman Bonesetter of Epsom are too many to be enumerated: Her Bandages are extraordinary Neat, and her Dexterity in reducing Dislocations and setting of fractured Bones wonderful. She has cured Persons who have been above 20 Years disabled, and has given incredible relief in the most difficult Cases.

This skill, passed on by her father, a 'bonesetter' of Hindon in Wiltshire, had once earned her the nickname 'Crazy Sally'. Then it gave her fame, fortune and a husband who married her for her money; Mr Mapp stayed with his wife for a fortnight and then ran off with a hundred guineas.

She lived at Epsom but is thought to have died in lodgings somewhere near Seven Dials in London, poor and forgotten. Perhaps the memory of a song comforted her a little:

> You Surgeons of London who puzzle your Pates,
> To ride in your Coaches, and purchase Estates,
> Give over, for Shame, for your pride has a Fall,
> And ye Doctress of Epsom has outdone you all.

JANE MARCET

1769–1858
(née Haldimand)
Died: Stratton Street, W1

Jane's father was a wealthy Swiss merchant who had settled in London. In 1799 she married Dr Marcet, physician and experimental chemist. It was with his help and advice that she broke into what was an entirely new field – writing simple text books, for young people, on scientific subjects. Most of her books had the title 'Conversations' – her *Conversations on Chemistry* was published in 1806, and the popular *Conversations on Political Economy* was much admired by Harriet Martineau (q.v.), herself a political economist.

Jane Marcet's style was clear and friendly, the subjects she chose well researched and presented, and she succeeded in making them understandable and popular. Her works soon became used as text books in a large number of schools. She died in London.

SARAH CHURCHILL, DUCHESS OF MARLBOROUGH

1660–1744
(née Jennings)
Died: Marlborough House, The Mall, SW1

When she was thirteen, Sarah Jennings became a maid of honour to the Duchess of York. As such, she was also the companion and playfellow of the Duchess's younger daughter, Princess Anne. They became close friends and the friendship lasted for nearly thirty years. Sarah married John Churchill in 1678 and so later became Duchess of Marlborough. Anne married Prince George of Denmark and, in 1702, became Queen Anne.

Sarah was beautiful, brilliant, impatient, tactless and ambitious. Her husband, Commander-in-Chief of the British army, earned the respect and gratitude of the British nation by his victories at Blenheim, Ramillies and Oudenarde. Anne was ordinary, overweight, unimaginative and stubborn. Her husband was insignificant. The Queen and the Duchess eventually quarrelled so bitterly that they never spoke to each other again.

Sarah disliked Blenheim Palace, built in her husband's honour, and quarrelled with the architect, John Vanbrugh but her husband adored her and after his death she refused the proposal of the Duke of Somerset, saying:

> If I were young and handsome as I was, instead of old and faded as I am, and you could lay the empire of the world at my feet, you should never share the heart and hand that once belonged to John, Duke of Marlborough.

She died at her home in London (Marlborough House) but was buried, with her husband, in the chapel at Blenheim Palace.

HARRIET MARTINEAU

1802–1876
Lived: Conduit Street, W1

My first political interest was the death of Nelson. I was then four years old. My father came in from the counting-house at an unusual hour, and told my mother, who cried heartily.

Born in Norwich, Harriet had already written *Illustrations of Political Economy* and become the bread-winner of the family before she moved to London. Invited to visit the USA, she published *Society in America* in 1837 and her only novel, *Deerbrook*, in 1839. She worked tremendously hard, producing forty-five books on subjects ranging from education and religion to the abolition of slavery and hypnotism, and became renowned as a political economist, reformer and feminist. Under the strain of work, combined with her struggle to conform to Victorian attitudes towards women, her health broke down. Convinced, in 1855, that she was dying, she hurriedly wrote her autobiography, but lived for another twenty years. Most of her life she was severely handicapped by acute deafness and Jane Carlyle (q.v.) once wrote of her:

They may call her what they please, but it is plain to me and to everybody of common sense . . . that she is distinctly good-looking, warm-hearted even to a pitch of romance, witty as well as wise, very entertaining and entertainable in spite of the deadening and killing appendage of an ear-trumpet. . . .

Living later in Ambleside (Cumbria), Harriet continued to contribute articles on social and political reform to various periodicals and, in 1855, published her *Complete Guide to the Lakes*. She was buried in Birmingham and her *Autobiographical Memoirs* was published posthumously.

ELEANOR MARX

1855–1898
Born: 28 Dean Street, Soho, W1 (Plaque to Karl Marx);
Buried: Highgate Cemetery (East), Swains Lane, N6

The greatest tragedy, as it seems to me, is that when she came to her end – and she had a right to choose that end – she did not realise how much she had come to be loved and honoured in the movement. (E. P. Thompson, *New Society*, 1977)

Karl Marx and his wife had three daughters, Jenny, Laura and Eleanor. The youngest, Eleanor, nicknamed 'Tussy' by the family, was born in Soho, London. It is said that the eldest, Jenny, was her father's favourite, but Marx once remarked: 'Jenny is most like me, but Tussy is me.'

A loyal disciple of her father, Eleanor became passionately involved in most of the political issues of the time. She studied, taught, travelled, translated and lectured on social and political subjects, eventually joining the executive of the Social Democratic Federation. Always interested in the position of women in society she created and worked for the first women's branch of the Gasworkers' Union. She was also an enthusiastic amateur actress and a member of the 'New Shakespeare Society'.

Eleanor lived for many years with Edward Aveling, doctor, lecturer, journalist and fellow-socialist. Most of her friends disliked him intensely, considering him to be cold, calculating and untrustworthy. Superficially brilliant, and attractive to many women, he was a compulsive womaniser, incapable of giving Eleanor the security and warm affection she hoped for. She continued to love him, and live with him, but her self-confidence was slowly and painfully undermined.

In 1895, with a legacy left to her by her father's old friend, Frederick Engels, she bought a house called 'The Den' in Jews Walk, Sydenham and moved in with Aveling. In June 1897 he secretly married a young woman called Eva Frye and in August that year he left Eleanor. Incredibly, he returned to live with her almost immediately. It has been suggested that he found he could not manage without Eleanor's money.

In March 1898 Eleanor Marx committed suicide by swallowing prussic acid. Her body was cremated at Woking and the ashes eventually buried in her parents' grave in Highgate Cemetery.

> I'd rather be a kitten and cry mew than a woman trying to earn a living. (Eleanor Marx to her sister Laura, 1885)

MARY, ('THE FERRY-MAN'S DAUGHTER')

(of Southwark)
possibly ninth century
Southwark Cathedral, SE1

Southwark Cathedral, on the south side of London Bridge, is officially 'The Cathedral and Collegiate Church of St Saviour and St Mary Overie'. Although rebuilt in the nineteenth century, it has a very long history.

According to John Stow (the sixteenth-century London historian), Mary, a local ferry-owner's daughter, founded a house of sisters there 'long before the Conquest . . . where now standeth the east part of St Mary Overies church, above the choir'. She inherited the ferry business, left all the profits to the nunnery, and was buried there when she died.

An extraordinary story survives about Mary's family. It is said that her father decided to test their affection by feigning his own death. To his horror, instead of tears and grief there was great rejoicing and his dear ones held a feast to celebrate. Boiling with rage, he stalked in upon the assembled company. A boat-man (understandably thinking he was seeing a ghost) hit him with an oar . . . and killed him.

It is reasonable to assume that Mary felt a little strange about the circumstances of her father's death and her resultant inheritance. Perhaps she founded the nunnery as a penance.

QUEEN MATILDA

1102–1167
Lodged: near Westminster Abbey

Granddaughter of William the Conqueror and daughter of Henry I, Matilda was educated in England. When she was eight years old she was betrothed to the German Emperor, Henry V, and sent to Germany. In 1114 she was formally married to him and became the Empress Matilda.

When she was eighteen her two brothers died, drowned at sea in the *White Ship*. When she was twenty-two her husband died. In 1126 she set sail for England, where her father insisted that she be accepted as his heir and Queen of England after his death. Matilda was then married off (very reluctantly) to Geoffrey of Anjou and gave birth to two sons. In 1135 her father died.

Rumours were circulated that Henry had changed his mind on his death-bed. Matilda's cousin, Stephen, claimed succession to the crown of England. The barons were unwilling to accept a woman as Queen and the Pope, diplomatically, accepted Stephen's claim. Civil war broke out in England. Matilda, having given birth to a third son, began to raise an army . . . her forces landed at Arundel in 1139.

By 1141 Stephen had lost the battle of Lincoln and Matilda held the balance of power. She began the 'acceptance' of the country, but failed disastrously in London. Having refused to reduce taxes, she was considered arrogant and offended too many powerful people. The City, aided by Stephen's wife and her followers, rose against Matilda and she was forced to flee. Finally, besieged at Oxford Castle, it is said that she escaped by dressing in white and stealing through the enemy lines during a snowstorm.

Defeated, she left England and settled in Rouen. Her eldest son succeeded to the English throne after Stephen's death and became Henry II. Matilda died in Rouen and was buried in the Abbey of Bec.

> Here lies Henry's Daughter,
> Mother, Wife,
> Great in all three: her son the Glory
> of her life.

HARRIOT MELLON

d. 1837
(Coutts, and then
Duchess of St Albans)
Holly Lodge Gardens, N6

In 1795 Harriot Mellon appeared in London as Lydia Languish in Sheridan's *The Rivals*. Charles Macklin, the actor, described her as: '. . . blooming in complexion, with a very tall, fine figure, raven locks . . . all she put you in mind of was a country road and a pillion . . .'

The wealthy banker, Thomas Coutts, depressed by his wife's mental illness, met this vision of health and loveliness and took her under his protection. By 1808, Harriot was installed in Holly Lodge, near Highgate Village, where she lived in style and became contentedly plump. Mrs Coutts died in 1815 and Thomas secretly married Harriot in St Pancras Church. When he finally plucked up the courage to tell his daughters, they were horrified and made embarrassing scenes.

Harriot, unabashed, made friends with his grandchildren.

Thomas Coutts died in 1822, leaving his whole estate to Harriot 'for her sole use and benefit' and making her a partner in the bank. He also left it to her to decide who should succeed her. Some years later (married to the Duke of St Albans) she began to take an increasing interest in her first husband's granddaughter, Angela Burdett, and would invite this shy, serious girl to various balls and dinners at Holly Lodge.

When she died it was discovered that Harriot had left almost everything to the twenty-three-year-old Angela – providing that she took the surname 'Coutts' (q.v.), and also providing that she did not marry a foreigner!

ADAH ISAAC MENKEN

c. 1864
(née McCord)
Asked to leave a hotel in St James's Street, SW1
(For unseemly and riotous conduct)

Having learned to ride at Franconi's Circus in New York, acted a little, written a little, and having divorced her husband (although she kept his name), Adah Menken sailed for England. She was employed by E. T. Smith, and appeared at Astley's Circus, London, in 1864 as 'Mazeppa' in an act based on wild-horse riding. Thomas Frost, in his *Circus Life and Circus Celebrities* (1875) described the publicity:

> Enormous posters everywhere met the eye, representing the lady, apparently in a nude state, stretched on the back of a wild horse, and inviting the public to go to Astley's and see 'the beautiful Menken'. Young men thronged the theatre to witness this combination of 'poses plastiques' with dramatic spectacle, and 'girls of the period' dressed their hair 'à la Menken' . . . but the theatrical critics looked coldly and sadly upon the performance, and accused the management of ministering to a vitiated taste.

Undaunted, Adah published a volume of poetry while she was in London, titled *Infelicia* and dedicated to Charles Dickens. For a short while she also became the mistress of the poet, Algernon Charles Swinburne. According to Julian Osgood Field, in his gossipy *Things I Shouldn't Tell* (1925), Adah died in Paris, after a particularly wild party where everyone drank 'oceans of brandy'. She was buried in the Père Lachaise cemetery there.

ALICE MEYNELL

1847–1922
(née Thompson)
Buried: St Mary's Catholic Cemetery, Kensal Green, NW10;
Plaque: 47 Palace Court, W2

Alice Meynell was a journalist, essayist and a gifted poet:

> On London fell a clearer light;
> Caressing pencils of the sun
> Defined the distances, the white
> Houses transfigured one by one,
> The 'long, unlovely street'
>   impearled.
> Oh, what a sky has walked the
>   world!

After her marriage to Wilfrid Meynell in 1877, Alice spent most of the rest of her life in London.

Effie Millais lived at 2 Palace Gate, W8

KATE MEYRICK

d. 1933
Site of 43 Club, Gerrard Street, W1

Most of my dance hostesses have been girls of the finest type in every sense. Many have formed in my clubs a stepping-stone to a happy marriage – some with peers of the realm, some with American millionaires, some with rich young men about Town, some with just ordinary good fellows . . . (Kate Meyrick, *Secrets of the 43*)

Kate, deserted by her husband and with a family to bring up, became a night-club owner. In 1921 she bought 43 Gerrard Street in Soho and so began the No. 43 Club. Another of her successes was the 'Silver Slipper Club', resplendent with a glass floor, in Regent Street.

Inevitably she clashed with the police, mostly over after-hours drinking, and in 1924 was sentenced to six months in Holloway Prison. Her clubs remained as popular as ever with the 'Bright Young Things' of the 20s. She wrote her reminiscences, which were published the year she died under the title *Secrets of the 43*. The book, however, gives the strong impression that she kept far more secrets than she gave away!

EFFIE (EUPHEMIA) MILLAIS

1828–1897
(née Gray)
Plaque: 2 Palace Gate, W8

In 1848, Effie Gray married the art critic, John Ruskin; their marriage was not consummated. She told no one but endeavoured to enjoy their travel and social life. Understandably, she suffered symptoms of nervous tension, which were aggravated by a difficult relationship with her in-laws.

In 1853 she sat for her husband's friend, John Millais, the pre-Raphaelite painter, for his painting 'The Order of Release' (now in the Tate Gallery) and the same year, Effie, Ruskin, Millais and his brother set off together for a tour of Scotland. When Ruskin sprained his ankle they stopped at Brig O'Turk and rented a cottage there.

Millais decided to start work on a portrait of Ruskin standing by a rocky stream; he also gave Effie drawing lessons and made numerous sketches of her. Ruskin seemed to leave them alone together deliberately, and they gradually became more and more involved. Deeply disturbed on her return to London, Effie wrote to her parents and told them the truth about her marriage. In 1854 they took her home to Scotland with them, Ruskin went abroad, and the marriage was annulled.

Effie married John Millais the following year. They had eight children and lived in London, in Cromwell Place and at 2 Palace Gate, near Kensington Gardens. When she died, she was buried in the old graveyard of Kinnoul on the banks of the Tay, in Scotland.

LADY MARY WORTLEY MONTAGU

1689–1762
(née Pierrepont)
Buried: Grosvenor Chapel, South Audley Street, W1 (unmarked)

To say truth, there is no part of the world where our sex is treated with so much contempt as in England.

Daughter of the first Duke of Kingston and sometimes described as the first blue-stocking, Mary was born in London. Her mother died when she was very young; brought up by her father, she taught herself Latin, was soon writing poetry and developed into an independent young woman. When her father rejected Edward Wortley Montagu as a suitor she slipped off and married him.

While in Constantinople (Edward having been made

Ambassador to the Porte), Mary noted the Turkish custom of inoculation for smallpox, studied it carefully, and had her son inoculated. Her efforts to introduce the practice in England met with much opposition.

Eccentric, involved in scandal, accused of political intrigue, Lady Mary continued to write (publishing anonymously). Her letters, mainly written while she was living in Italy, are a delight. She made many close friends, some bitter enemies (one of them Alexander Pope), and left her husband before she was fifty. After extensive travel she returned in 1761, 'dragging my ragged remnant of life to England', to live in Mayfair. She died of cancer.

LOLA MONTEZ

d. 1861
(née Gilbert)
Lived: Half Moon Street, off Piccadilly, W1

Lola (or Marie Dolores Eliza Rosanna) Gilbert was born in Ireland. Threatened with marriage to an elderly judge, she ran away with a young lieutenant, Thomas James, married him and accompanied him to India. It soon became clear that their marriage was a failure and she was sent back to England. En route she met a dashing Captain who deserted her after a brief affair and Lola was left to her own devices. So began her apprenticeship as an adventuress.

Having spent a little time in Madrid where she had learned to dance rather badly in the Spanish style, she appeared in 1843 at Her Majesty's Theatre in London. As 'Donna Lola Montez of the Teatro Real, Seville', she danced 'El Oleano' in between the acts of *The Barber of Seville*. Her figure, face and flair were well received and, encouraged by her success, she made a second appearance at Covent Garden and then set off to conquer the world. She visited Belgium and Berlin and had a stormy affair with Franz Liszt. In Paris, where her dancing was *not* appreciated, she took off her garters and threw them disdainfully at the audience. She cultivated a tempestuous image,

using a horsewhip if insulted and firing pistols when annoyed.

In 1846 she reached Munich and captivated Ludwig, the King of Bavaria:

> She was by him raised to the rank of the Countess of Lansfelt, but interfering in political matters, she was driven from the country, and her royal protector thought it advisable to abdicate the throne. (*The Gentleman's Magazine*, 1861)

Returning to London, Lola married George Heald, a Cornet in the Life Guards, but, as her first husband was still alive, she was arrested for bigamy and the case was heard at Marlborough Street Police Court. Although they fled abroad and travelled around together, they spent most of their time quarrelling bitterly, and George Heald eventually returned to England.

Lola Montez, having toured America, married again, visited Australia, written her autobiography and flourished her whip on a few more occasions, finally settled in New York. She died there, full of repentance, and was buried in Greenwood Cemetery as 'Mrs Eliza Gilbert'.

HANNAH MORE

1745–1833
Drury Lane Theatre, Catherine Street, WC2

Well educated by their father (a schoolmaster), Hannah and her four sisters successfully ran a school for 'young ladies' in Bristol for many years. Then Hannah agreed to marry a Mr Turner, almost twice her age. When their engagement was, reluctantly, broken off, he insisted on giving her an annuity, thus making her independent.

She spent a great deal of time visiting London, where she met, and became friendly with, Sir Joshua Reynolds, Dr Johnson, Horace Walpole and the circle of intellectual women known as the 'blue-stockings'. A frequent visitor at David Garrick's house, and a close friend of his wife, she also wrote several plays. One of them, *Percy*, was performed at Drury Lane Theatre for fourteen successive nights – in those days considered a good run.

At the age of forty Miss More retreated from London and lived in a cottage at Wrington, Somerset, with her sisters. They set up schools in the district, established festivals and worked to improve conditions in the surrounding area. Their strongly-held and independent religious views were not always appreciated by the local clergy – or magistrates. Hannah continued to write, and when she was over eighty moved to Clifton, outside Bristol. She was buried in the churchyard at Wrington.

LADY OTTOLINE MORRELL

1873–1938
(née Cavendish-Bentinck)
Lived: 44 Bedford Square, WC1

Ottoline had a great influence upon me, which was almost wholly beneficial. She laughed at me when I behaved like a don or a prig, and when I was dictatorial in conversation. (Bertrand Russell)

Married to Philip Morrell (later MP for South Oxfordshire) in 1902, Lady Ottoline became the friend, hostess and benefactress of many young intellectuals of the day, including Bertrand Russell – with whom she had an affair – Joseph Conrad, Aldous Huxley, D. H. Lawrence and Virginia and Leonard Woolf. Somewhat bizarre in her choice of dress and style of living, she is said to have inspired the character of Hermione Roddice in D. H. Lawrence's *Women in Love*. If this is so, it was a cruel betrayal of her generosity towards the author.

Lady Ottoline Morrell helped to found what is now the Contemporary Art Society. She was buried in Holbeck Church on the Welbeck estate, in Nottinghamshire.

ETHEL LE NEVE

1883–1967
Lived: 39 Hilldrop Crescent, N7 (House no longer exists)

What I have suffered during the last few months no one can guess.

Ethel le Neve's lover, Dr Crippen, murdered his wife, Belle Elmore, and buried her dismembered remains in the cellar of their home, 39 Hilldrop Crescent. He then announced that his wife had left him and gone to America. Quite soon Ethel moved into the house with him. It seems she did not find it at all strange that Belle had left all her clothes and jewellery behind. Others, however, were more suspicious and had approached the police. Enquiries were set in motion and Dr Crippen was interviewed, but by the time the police felt they had a case, and arrived at Hilldrop Crescent, the birds had flown. Belle's grisly remains were discovered and the hunt was on.

Ethel, disguised as a boy, and Dr Crippen, posing as a merchant, had boarded a cargo ship, the *Montrose*, bound for Canada. The captain sensed something was wrong, guessed their identities and contacted the ship-owners in England by radio-telegraph. Inspector Dew, of Scotland Yard, set off in pursuit in a faster ship, and on 31 July 1910 he boarded the *Montrose*. Dr Crippen and Ethel were arrested, taken back to London, and tried. Crippen was condemned to death and later executed. Ethel was found not guilty of being an accessory after the fact, and released.

Ethel le Neve, Her Life Story; With the True Account of their Flight and her Friendship for Dr Crippen, Told by Herself was published shortly after the trial:

> Little more than three months ago I was an obscure typist, earning my living like thousands of other girls in the City. All I wished was happiness, not notoriety . . .

Ethel le Neve lived in America for a while, but returned to England and married. It is said she died in Dulwich.

Florence Nightingale's statue in Waterloo Place, SW1. 'I stand at the altar of murdered men, And while I live I fight their cause'

FLORENCE NIGHTINGALE

1820–1910
Plaque: 10 South Street,
W1;
Crimean War Memorial,
Waterloo Place, SW1

Born in Italy, brought up in England, buried in the churchyard of St Margaret of Antioch, East Wellow, Hampshire, Florence Nightingale became a heroine during her lifetime and a legend after her death.

In London there is a statue of her by Mancini on the terrace of St Thomas's Hospital, where she founded a school of nursing. At the intersection of Pall Mall and Waterloo Place she is represented in the Crimean War Memorial, and in the crypt of St Paul's Cathedral there is a commemorative plaque to her.

As a child she was introspective, as a teenager she found the glamour of social life unattractive. By the time she was thirty, having turned down a proposal of marriage, Florence could find little to make life worth living. Then, ignoring her family's disapproval, she studied at Kaiserworth Hospital in Germany and at the Maison de la Providence in Paris. On her return to England, she became Superintendent at the Institution for the Care of Sick Gentlewomen in Distressed Circumstances, and it was there that she revealed an outstanding ability for organisation.

In January 1854 war broke out in the Crimea, and in April the first detachment of troops left England. Newspaper reports soon told of appalling conditions suffered by the sick and wounded and the British public were suitably shocked. Sydney Herbert, the Secretary at War, decided to send his friend Miss Nightingale out there.

In November 1854, accompanied by thirty-eight nurses, she arrived at Constantinople and proceeded to the Barracks Hospital at Scutari. No beds had been provided for them, no food and little water. The hospital staff were hostile. The nurses watched, helplessly, as an endless procession of wounded arrived from the Battle of Balaclava but the system began to break down under the strain, and they were finally allowed to play their part. Florence Nightingale took over.

She received the sick, deployed her nurses, wrote reports, ironed out problems of organisation and superintended the care of the wounded and dying. By May she had improved conditions beyond belief. Although she fell seriously ill she refused to go home until July 1856. On her return she campaigned for a Royal Commission to report on the health of the army and, when it was set up, wrote her own notes for it. In 1859 she published her *Notes on Nursing*, and a year later founded the school of nursing at St Thomas's Hospital. Then came her work on the army in India and involvement in hospital reform, the workhouse system, the Poor Law reform and childbirth statistics.

Florence Nightingale settled in a house in South Street, Mayfair, in London. When she was offered the Order of Merit in 1907 she is said to have muttered, 'Too kind – too kind!'. She was ninety-one when she died.

HELENA NORMANTON, QC

1883–1957
(Mrs Clark)
Middle Temple, EC4

The first prisoner to be defended by a woman barrister at the Old Bailey was acquitted yesterday. He . . . had picked Mrs Helena Normanton to represent him under the impression that he was choosing a counsel of his own sex . . . (*Daily Telegraph*, February 1924)

Having gained first class honours in Modern History at London University, Helena Normanton was admitted as a law student at the Middle Temple in 1919. She was called to the Bar in 1922 and briefed in the High Court in the same year. Married to Gavin Clark, she fought to preserve her maiden name professionally, became the first woman to be elected to the General Council of the Bar and, at the same time as Rose Heilbron, (now Judge of the High Court of Justice) was made a King's Counsel in 1949.

MARIANNE NORTH

1830–1890
The Marianne North Gallery, Kew Gardens, Richmond, Surrey

The Marianne North Gallery, in Kew Gardens, was first opened to the public in 1882. It was designed by James Fergusson under the supervision of the artist, whose 832 botanical paintings cover its walls today.

For years Marianne travelled the world with her adored father, exploring, painting, and sometimes discovering new specimens that were named after her. In between journeys she lived in a flat in Victoria Street, London.

Her paintings are strong, colourful, confident, showing an imagination stirred by the drama of exotic surroundings. In her autobiography *Recollections of a Happy Life* her words often echo this joy in visual experience:

> We were soon amongst the mysterious festoons of floating gulfweed. Even the sea-water was warm, and it looked such a solid black blue, and the weed as gold or amber on it, with the long streaks of floating white foam over all.

She retired to Alderley, Gloucestershire, and was buried in the churchyard there.

CAROLINE NORTON

1808–1877
(née Sheridan)
Married: St George's Church, Hanover Square

Caroline was a granddaughter of the playwright Richard Brinsley Sheridan. Her marriage to George Norton in 1827 (at the church of St George's, Hanover Square, London) was an abysmal failure. Not only were their political opinions totally at odds, but George tended to use physical violence when angry. Caroline, lonely and unhappy, began to develop an interest in literature and published, anonymously, a poem called *The Sorrows of Rosalie* in 1829. She also gave birth to their first child.

Among her many friends and admirers was Lord Melbourne (a political enemy of her husband) to whom she was greatly attracted. Gossip soon began to link their names together. Before the birth of their third child, the Nortons' marriage had reached a crisis and, in 1836, they separated publicly. George took the children away from her, refused her any provision and brought a suit against Lord Melbourne for the alienation of his wife's affections. Her acquittal was total, but her life had been ruined.

Caroline continued to write poetry, and novels. Allowed to have her children to stay with her for part of each year, she then began a struggle to reform the laws of marriage, divorce and custody. In the 1850s she met William Stirling of Keir and became very fond of him. However, he too was married and it was not until their mutual partners were dead that they married, in 1877. By that time Caroline was sixty-nine. She died, in London, in the same year.

> For death and life, in ceaseless strife,
> Beat wild on this world's shore,
> And all our calm is in that balm –
> Not lost but gone before.
> (Caroline Norton)

ANNE OLDFIELD

1683–1730
Buried: Westminster Abbey (South Aisle of Nave)

Actress and rival of Anne Bracegirdle (q.v.), she was much admired on stage. She also left two illegitimate sons, although it was rumoured that she had married the father, General Charles Churchill, of the second boy. Her funeral was magnificent and she was buried in all her finery, inspiring Pope's acid lines:

> 'Odious! in woollen! 'twould a saint provoke'
> (Were the last words that poor Narcissa spoke);
> 'No; let a charming chintz and Brussels lace
> Wrap my cold limbs and shade my lifeless face;
> One would not, sure, be frightful when one's dead –
> And, Betty, give this cheek a little red.'

BARONESS ORCZY

1865–1947
(Mrs Montague Barstow)
Temple Underground Station, EC4

. . . Strangely enough that personality of the Scarlet Pimpernel came to me in a very curious way. I first saw him standing before me – don't gasp, please – on the platform of an underground station, the Temple . . . Now, of all the dull, prosy places in the world, can you beat an underground railway station? It was foggy too, and smelly and cold. But I give you my word that as I was sitting there, I saw – yes, I saw – Sir Percy Blakeney, just as you know him now. (Baroness Orczy, *Links in the Chain of Life*)

And (strangely enough) Baroness Orczy's first novel with the Scarlet Pimpernel as its hero was turned down by twelve publishers before he emerged to delight generations of fans.

Born in Hungary, she arrived in London at the age of fifteen and studied painting at the West London School of Art. However, after her marriage to Montague Barstow, she began to write and travel widely, spending most of the Second World War in the south of France. She died in London.

Baroness Orczy wrote many novels and a biography of the Duchesse de Berri [*The Turbulent Duchess*] but it was Sir Percy Blakeney who made her famous and to whom she gave a life of his own:

> We seek him here, we seek him there,
> Those Frenchies seek him everywhere.
> Is he in Heaven? – Is he in Hell?
> That demmed, elusive Pimpernel.

DOROTHY OSBORNE

1627–1695
(Lady Temple)
Tablet: South Aisle, Westminster Abbey

Letters have often been written that later become either part of a nation's history, or part of its literature. Dorothy Osborne's love letters to William Temple, although they have been published, edited, studied and analysed, are not so easily classified.

Born at Chicksands, near Bedford, of a staunchly 'Royalist' family, Dorothy grew up to be an attractive but retiring and even slightly melancholy young woman. When she and William Temple first met they were immediately attracted to each other. However, both families disapproved of the match, and they were parted. Years of frustration, disappointment and even despair followed. Finally, in 1654, they were able to marry.

Dorothy's letters span only a short period of her life before the marriage, but they illuminate with great charm the thoughts and feelings of an otherwise ordinary young woman living in the seventeenth century. Perhaps she herself provides the explanation for her own ability:

> All letters methinks should be free and easy as one's discourse, not studied as an oration, nor made up of hard words like a charm. 'Tis an admirable thing to see how some people will labour to find out terms that may obscure a plain sense; like a gentleman I knew who would never say 'The weather grew cold', but that 'Winter began to salute us'.

Very little is known of her after she became Temple's wife.

DAME ALICE OWEN

1547–1613
(née Wilkes)
St Mary's Church, N1

Walking across her father's fields in Islington, young Alice Wilkes decided to try her hand at milking. As she stood up, a stray arrow from the nearby archery range pierced her tall hat, missing her head by inches. She promptly vowed that one day she would build something there to commemorate her deliverance and the Lord's mercy.

In 1608, three marriages and twelve children later, Dame Alice Owen bought 'Ermitage Fields', Islington, and had almshouses for 'ten poor old widows' built there. Later, with more land, and the Worshipful Company of Brewers as trustees, a royal patent allowed her to put up more buildings including 'one chapel and house for . . . one good man, who may be able to read to the aforesaid widows . . . and teach the sons and daughters of the poor'. Before she died, Alice had issued 'orders and rules' for the running of the new school opened for thirty poor boys (the poor girls had to wait until 1886!).

The Dame Alice Owen school moved to Potters Bar after 1973; a statue of her stands in the dining hall. She was buried in St Mary's church, Islington Green, but the old church was rebuilt in 1751 and restored again in 1962.

There is a pub called the Lady Owen Arms in Goswell Road, Islington – strangely, the sign outside it portrays a sixteenth-century *man*!

Statues of Dame Alice Owen stand in the entrance and dining halls at the Owen School, Potters Bar

DAME MARY PAGE

1672–1728
Buried: Bunhill Fields,
EC1

IN 67 MONTHS SHE WAS TAPD 66 TIMES
HAD TAKEN AWAY 240 GALLONS OF WATER
WITHOUT EVER REPINING AT HER CASE
OR EVER FEARING THE OPERATION

The entrance to Bunhill Fields is opposite Wesley's Chapel in the City Road. It was used as a Non-Conformist burial ground between 1623 and 1852 and John Bunyan, Daniel Defoe and William and Catherine Blake are buried there.

So is the unknown but heroic Mary Page:

Here lyes Dame Mary Page
Relict of Sir Gregory Page Bart
She departed this life March 4 1728
In the 56th year of her age.
In 67 months she was Tap'd 66 times
Had taken away 240 Gallons of Water
Without ever repining at her case
Or ever fearing the operation.

DAME CHRISTABEL PANKHURST

1880–1958
Memorial: Victoria
Tower Gardens, SW1

At Manchester University, Christabel Pankhurst took the LL.B. degree and won a prize for International Law, but when she sought admission as a student for Lincoln's Inn she was refused. With her mother, Emmeline Pankhurst (q.v.), she helped to found the Women's Social and Political Union (WSPU) and soon became a committed militant in the suffrage movement.

She was arrested, with Annie Kenney (q.v.), in 1905, for interrupting a political meeting (and, it is said, spitting at the policeman who arrested her). In 1907, arrested again, she was tried and charged with inciting to riot. During the trial, she used her right to cross-examine and made H. Gladstone, (the Home Secretary) and Lloyd George (then Chancellor of the Exchequer) quite

uncomfortable. At the peak of the militant action she was forced to flee abroad and, for a while, directed operations from Paris.

Christabel later stood for Parliament but was narrowly defeated at Smethwick. In 1936 she was made Dame Commander of the British Empire. She became deeply religious, lived in America for many years, preaching the imminence of the Second Advent and died in Los Angeles. The following year her memorial was added to that of her mother in the Victoria Tower Gardens, near the House of Lords. Two low curving walls enclose Mrs Pankhurst's statue; at the end of one is a bronze medallion of Christabel, at the end of the other, a replica of the 'prison' brooch worn by imprisoned members of the WSPU.

EMMELINE PANKHURST

1858–1928
(née Goulden)
Statue: Victoria Tower
Gardens, SW1

Emmeline Pankhurst's
grave in Brompton
Cemetery

I am what you call a hooligan!
(Emmeline Pankhurst 1909)

The suffragette movement and the name of Pankhurst are inseparable: Emmeline's statue stands in Victoria Tower Gardens, by the House of Lords; she looks both elegant and cheerfully resigned. Is this the woman who threw stones at the windows of 10 Downing Street? Who was arrested, at the age of fifty-six, outside Buckingham Palace and had to be carried away, kicking and shouting? 'Nothing,' said Emmeline once, 'has ever been got out of the British parliament without something approaching a revolution.'

Born in Manchester, she married a known radical, Dr Richard Pankhurst, and had five children. They moved to London in 1886 and Emmeline developed her

interest in politics and women's franchise. After her husband's death in 1898, and now totally committed to 'Votes for Women', she was the moving spirit behind the Women's Social and Political Union, gradually becoming more and more militant until she was arrested for the first time in 1908. Falling ill in a cold cell, she was released, only to rush off to a packed and enthusiastic meeting at the Albert Hall.

Some suffragists disapproved of her methods but the 1914–18 war interrupted all their efforts. Mrs Pankhurst lived to see a Bill passed allowing women over thirty to vote and as she lay dying in 1928, the Bill for full equal suffrage was being approved in the House of Lords. She was buried in Brompton Cemetery.

Statue of Emmeline Pankhurst in Victoria Tower Gardens, Westminster. 'Nothing has ever been got out of a British Parliament without something approaching a revolution'

SYLVIA PANKHURST

1882–1960
Lived Cheyne Walk, SW3
also Notting Hill Gate,
W11

A daughter of Emmeline Pankhurst (q.v.), Sylvia was greatly attracted to the visual arts. She studied in both Venice and Florence (having won a travelling scholarship from Manchester School of Art) and at the Royal College of Art in London.

Being a Pankhurst, she naturally became involved in the Suffragette movement – and was imprisoned for a while in Holloway – but spent most of her time designing cards, posters and banners for the Women's Social and Political Union. She also painted portraits of ordinary women 'at work' and in 1909 designed the decorations for the hall where a Women's Exhibition was to be held.

After a disagreement with her sister, Christabel (q.v.), over suffrage policy, Sylvia moved towards more socialist reforms, and became particularly active in the East End of London. She was imprisoned again, several times, and forcibly fed.

After the birth of her son, Richard, in 1927 (she did not marry), Sylvia became interested in international politics, particularly the cause of Ethiopia against the fascist invasion, and edited the *New Times and Ethiopia News*. Having visited Ethiopia she decided to settle in Addis Ababa. She died and was buried in the Selassie, or 'Trinity', cathedral there.

ANN PARKER

fl. 1797
(née MacHardy)
Queen Street, EC4 and
Whitechapel Road, E1

Ann married Richard Parker in 1791. Later he 'volunteered' for the navy and, in March 1797, was sent to the Nore, on board the flagship *Sandwich*. Seamen's pay was poor, their food atrocious . . . that year they mutinied. The red flag of defiance was hoisted aboard the *Sandwich* and other mutinous ships. Richard Parker was elected President of the Committee of Delegates and took part in negotiations with the Lords of the Admiralty. The mutiny failed and Parker was tried and sentenced to death.

Ann only wanted to see her husband before he died. An attempt to present a petition to the Queen was ignored. She set off to Rochester, where she persuaded a boatman to take her to Sheerness and alongside the *Sandwich*, but when she asked for permission to speak to her husband, they threatened to fire on her boat.

At her third attempt Ann witnessed the 'fatal procession of her husband from the quarter-deck to the forecastle', and fainted. Recovering, she then saw him 'mount the platform on the cat-head, and the clergyman . . . go from him'. From that moment she saw 'nothing but the sea, which appeared covered with blood'. They took her back to shore.

Her request for her husband's corpse having been refused, Ann made her way to the burial-ground and found some women to help her. Together, they climbed the fence, removed the earth that covered the coffin, somehow managed to get it over the gate – and together they sat on it until a fish-cart passed by. The driver was persuaded to take Ann and the coffin to Rochester, where she made arrangements to have it taken to London and placed at the Hoop and Horseshoe Tavern in Queen Street.

Word spread, crowds gathered . . . they were sympathetic. Ann was taken before the magistrates, where she explained that she only wanted 'to take him . . . either to his own family at Exeter or to hers in Scotland'. Accused of having 'suffered him to be shewn for money' she replied, in floods of tears, 'Do I appear like a monster so unnatural?'

At first they ordered that the body should be buried in Aldgate churchyard, then, 'apprehensive that some disaffected persons might be inclined to make the funeral a spectacle for the purposes of tumult', they switched the burial to a different church (Whitechapel) and a different time. Ann was allowed to go there and see him for the last time.

EMILY PARKER

fl. 1875
London Bridge, EC4

In October 1875, the *Englishwomen's Review* reported what was for those days a rare occurrence:

> ANOTHER LONG SWIM
> Miss Emily Parker started from London Bridge at 5.3 to swim to North Woolwich, a distance of ten miles. The tide was moderately good, but the wind was dead against the swimmer, making the water at times very rough and lumpy, and the constant breaking of the waves distressed her considerably. She, however, arrived safely at Woolwich at 7.26, and was carried into North Woolwich Gardens, where Mr Holland afterwards presented her with a gold medal value ten guineas.

QUEEN KATHERINE PARR

c. 1514–1548
Chelsea Palace stood on land which is now Cheyne Walk, SW3

Divorced, beheaded, died,
Divorced, beheaded – survived.

Katherine Parr, sixth wife of Henry VIII, was the one who survived – although not for long. Born in London and highly educated, she had already been married and widowed when the King, lonely, disillusioned and ill, began to show an interest in her. They were married in 1543.

With intelligent affection Katherine won the trust of his children and supervised their education. She was also made regent during the King's absence in France. Only once did her partiality for church reform place her in serious danger. Supporters of the old faith, plotting her downfall, made charges against her, but the King refused to listen to them.

Henry VIII died in 1547. Six months later Katherine married the dashing, irresponsible Admiral Thomas Seymour, and Princess Elizabeth (q.v.) became part of their household in Chelsea. Katherine was soon pregnant, but her husband's tactless romps with the young Princess became embarrassing to everybody (except the High Admiral himself) and Elizabeth was sent away. Then Katherine moved to Sudeley Castle for the birth of the baby. She died of puerperal fever and was buried in the chapel there.

CORA PEARL

1835(?)–1886
(Emma Crouch)
Worked as a milliner in Regent Street, SW1

I have never deceived anybody, because I have never belonged to anybody.

One of the most colourful 'courtesans' of the nineteenth century, Cora Pearl spent most of her life in France, but was born in Plymouth and then educated at a convent school in Boulogne. She returned to England and lived with her grandmother in London, where, still a young girl, she was seduced by an elderly man. Of this incident she was to write later:

> The next morning I found myself by the side of the man in his bed. It was one more child ruined – wickedly, bestially. I have never pardoned men, neither this one nor the others who are not responsible for his act.

Her life in Paris, her numerous lovers and her escapades have been well recorded: from being served up, naked, at dinner, on a silver salver, to dancing the hornpipe on a carpet of orchids sent by an admirer. She spent a fortune and died in Paris in poverty, but Cora Pearl surely deserves to be remembered for the outrageous splendour of her defiance:

> She was, as I say, very ugly, and not at all amusing, except in her extravagance – as when she hired the Theatre des Bouffes, sent tickets to all her friends – and appeared as

Cupidon, almost nude; that is, with no clothing on worth mentioning, but covered from head to foot with jewels – literally so, for in one last extravagant gambol she threw

herself flat on her back and flung her legs up in the air to show the soles of her shoes that were one mass of diamonds. (*Uncensored Recollections*, Julian Osgood Field)

MARY HERBERT, COUNTESS OF PEMBROKE

1561–1621
(née Sidney)
Hampton Court Palace,
Hampton Court,
Kingston-upon-Thames

Mary was a great patron of the arts, an incomparable hostess and the beloved sister of Sir Philip Sidney. In 1575 she was invited by Elizabeth I to join the royal household in London, and two years later married the Earl of Pembroke. She wrote poetry, worked on translations and studied chemistry. Most of the great minds of the age were invited to her country home, Wilton House in Wiltshire.

Greatly mourned at her death, William Browne wrote an unusual epitaph for Mary Herbert:

Underneath this sable hearse
Lies the subject of all verse:
Sydney's sister, Pembroke's
   mother –
Death, ere thou kill'st such another
Fair, and good, and learned as she
Time will throw his dart at thee.
Marble pyles let no man raise
To her name, for after daies
Some kind woman born as she
Reading this, like Niobe
Shall turn marble and become
Both her mourner and her tomb.

She was buried in the Pembroke family vault in Salisbury Cathedral. There is no monument.

SIBEL PENNE

d. 1562
Monument: South Porch
of St Mary the Virgin
Church, Hampton,
Middlesex

Jane Seymour, Henry VIII's third wife, gave birth to a baby boy at Hampton Court Palace in 1537, and then died. The King, terrified of losing his son, hurriedly established a separate household, solely concerned with the welfare of the child, who had been christened Edward. Sir William Sidney was to be the Chamberlain and Sibel Penne, the little Prince's

nurse.

Sibel remained a great favourite of Prince Edward's as he grew up and Henry VIII, delighted by her affectionate care of his son, presented Mistress Penne and her husband with lands in Buckinghamshire. Many years later, she died of smallpox and was buried in the church at Hampton, a small village near Hampton Court Palace.

Sibel Penne's ghost is said to haunt the neighbourhood. The church where she had been buried was pulled down and rebuilt in 1829. One story relates that, soon after this, noises could be heard through a wall in the south-west wing of the Palace . . . the sound of a voice murmuring and the hum of a spinning-wheel. Investigating later in that area of the Palace, the then Board of Works found a small, undiscovered room, and, inside it, an old spinning-wheel! The ghost was promptly identified locally as that of Sibel Penne. Legend also has it that she lived in a cottage, still in existence, near Hampton Church. A stained glass window, showing Sibel and Prince Edward standing together, was designed and added to the cottage by the present owner.

ELIZABETH PEPYS

1640–1669
(née Marchant)
St Olave's Church, Hart
Street, EC3

In the little church of St Olave is one of the most charming memorials in the City of London. Elizabeth, alert and smiling, seems to be trying to look across at the bust of her husband, Samuel Pepys. They were married when she was only fifteen – and a 'portionless' girl, which suggests a love match. From Samuel's diary emerges a portrait of an attractive, lively wife, not always the ideal housewife:

> Being come to some angry words with my wife about neglecting the keeping of the house clean, I calling her beggar and she me pricklouse, which vexed me.

But full of fun and capable of giving her husband more than a pang of jealousy:

> Home, where I found my wife and the dancing-master alone above, not dancing but talking. Now so deadly full of jealousy I am that . . . I could not do any business possibly, but went out to my office.

She was a good cook, but Samuel was not always enthusiastic about her dress sense:

> Home to dinner, where my wife and I fell out, I being displeased with her cutting away a lace handkercher sewed about her neck down to her breasts almost, out of a belief, but without reason, that it is the fashion.

Elizabeth died, childless, before she was thirty. Samuel did not marry again.

ALICE PERRERS

c. 1370
West Smithfield, EC1

Dame Alice Perrers the King's concubine, as Lady of the Sun, rode from the Tower of London, through Cheape, accompanied by many lords and ladies, every lady leading a lord by his horse-bridle, till they came into West Smithfield, and then began a great joust, which endured seven days after. (John Stow's *Survey of London*)

Alice's origins are obscure but, by 1366, she had joined the household of Queen Philippa (wife of Edward III) as Lady of the Bedchamber. Just over two years later, the Queen died and Alice became the King's mistress, with enormous influence over him. She was granted the manor of Wendover (Buckinghamshire), as well as land in the area that is now Hammersmith, in London, and so became one of the wealthiest women in England. Probably to give her both status and respectability, she was married off to William de Windsor.

Edward III died, it is said, in her arms. It was also rumoured that she removed the rings from his fingers once he was dead. When Richard II succeeded to the throne Alice was tried and sentenced to banishment. The grounds for her punishment were so weak that the sentence was revoked and her lands merely transferred to her husband's name. She asked, in her will, to be buried in the church at Upminster and may well have been buried there.

KATHERINE PHILIPS

1631–1664
(née Fowler)
Fleet Street, EC4

Born in London, Katherine wrote poetry under the pseudonym of 'Orinda'. Her admirers capped it and she became known as 'The Matchless Orinda'. John Aubrey gives a delightful pen-portrait of her in his *Brief Lives*:

> Very good-natured; not at all high-minded; pretty fatt; not tall; read (red) pumpled face; wrote out verses in Innes, or Mottos in windowes in her table-booke.

Katherine married a Welshman and lived for a while in Wales. Returning to London, they lived in Fleet Street, where she died of smallpox. She was buried in the church of St Benet Sherehog, one of the many city churches destroyed by the Great Fire of 1666. Her collected poems appeared in 1667.

LAETITIA PILKINGTON

1712–1750
(née van Lewen)
St James's Street, SW1

Born in Dublin, Laetitia married Matthew Pilkington there in 1730. She later described his proposal:

> To my great surprise, I found Mr Pilkington with my father, his harpsichord placed in the parlour, which, with a cat and an owl, were all his worldly goods. He told me, with great rapture, that he was going for a ring and a licence to be married in the evening.

The young couple became friendly with Jonathan Swift, who encouraged their literary efforts. In 1737, divorced on the grounds of her adultery (which she denied), Laetitia could not face the resulting scandal and, leaving her children behind, fled to London. Here she attempted to earn her living by writing and led a precariously reputable existence until she was sent to prison for debt. A friend, Colley Cibber, the playwright, came to her rescue, collected money and obtained her release.

Laetitia then opened a shop in St James's Street, selling prints and pamphlets. She placed a notice in the window:

> Letters written here on any subject, except the law. Price twelve pence. Petitions also drawn at the same rate. Mem: Ready money, no trust.

Unfortunately the shop failed and she returned to Ireland where, still haunted by the past, her *Memoirs* became a justification of her life. She died in Dublin.

POCOHONTAS

d. 1617

Statue: Vincent Square,
SW1

In 1607, three English ships carrying settlers arrived off the coast of Virginia and so began the first colony of Jamestown. One of their leaders, Captain John Smith, was later captured by Indians, and his life saved by the Indian chief's young daughter, Pocohontas. Captain Smith was released, allowed to return to Jamestown and then went back to England.

A few years after this, Pocohontas herself was kidnapped by a Captain Samuel Argall and taken to Jamestown where she was adopted, baptised a Christian and taught to speak English. She was given the name Rebecca and, in 1614, married one of the settlers, John Rolfe. Two years later they

sailed for England with their baby son, Thomas. Pocohontas attracted a great deal of interest in London, where she was entertained by the Bishop of London and finally presented at court. As she was about to return home to Virginia she fell ill at Gravesend, died and was buried there.

There is a large statue of her at Gravesend, given by the people of Virginia and, until recently, one called 'La Belle Sauvage' by David McFall, in Red Lion Square in London. This is now in the foyer of the offices of Cassell Limited (who commissioned the statue), in Vincent Square, SW1.

BEATRIX POTTER
1866–1943
(Mrs Heelis)
Born: 2 Bolton Gardens, Kensington, SW5

A solitary and restricted childhood in Kensington turned Beatrix into a painfully shy girl. Holidays in Scotland aroused her interest in natural history, she was allowed to accompany her brother to art galleries, and spent hours in the London museums, sketching and doing water-colours.

In her mid-thirties she offered a small book called *The Tale of Peter Rabbit* to Frederick Warne and Co. Having first refused it, they changed their minds, suggesting coloured illustrations – and so began Beatrix Potter's contribution to the major delights of childhood. (Illustrations from *The Tale of the Tailor of Gloucester* now hang in the Tate Gallery.)

Her engagement to Norman Warne, bravely defying her parents, ended tragically when he died of leukaemia. Beatrix Potter left London to live at Near Sawrey, Cumbria, where she owned Hill Top Farm, marrying her solicitor in 1913. As Mrs Heelis she became a sheep-farmer and died there, in the countryside of Jemima Puddleduck and Mrs Tiggy-Winkle.

ANN RADCLIFFE
1764–1823
(née Ward)
Buried: in the area of St George's Fields, Bayswater, W2

One of the best of the so-called 'Gothic' novelists, Ann was born and lived in London, suffered from asthma and married the Proprietor of the *English Chronicle*. When she retired from public life, the unfounded – but typically Gothic – rumour circulated that she had gone mad!

The graveyard off the Bayswater Road where she was buried is now a nursery-school playground, old tombstones stacked against the walls. Ann's is probably among them. Her novel, *The Mysteries of Udolpho*, was first published in 1794. The following passage is typical of her style. The heroine, Emily de St Aubert, approaches the Castle of Udolpho, accompanied by its owner, the sinister Count Montoni:

Towards the close of day, the road wound into a deep valley. Mountains, whose shaggy steeps appeared to be inaccessible, almost surrounded it. The sun had just sunk below the top of the mountains . . . but his sloping rays touched with a yellow gleam the summits of the forest . . . and streamed in full splendour upon the towers and battlements of a castle that spread its extensive ramparts along the brow of a precipice above . . . 'There,' said Montoni, speaking for the first time in several hours, 'is Udolpho.'

MARY READ
d. 1720
No address traced so far

In 1724 a book called *A General History of the Robberies and Murders of the Most Notorious Pirates* was published. The author was a Captain Charles Johnson, better known as Daniel Defoe. Chapter VIII spoke 'Of Mary Read and Anne Bonney, the Female Pirates'.

Anne Bonney, an Irish girl, was born near Cork and, as far as is known, never visited London. Mary Read, however, did. Her mother, abandoned by her husband, was left not only with a small son to provide for, but also pregnant. The little boy died and a daughter, Mary, was born. Mary's mother dressed her as a boy, went to London, and presenting her mother-in-law with a 'grandson', claimed an allowance for him. The ruse was successful. Mary was kept in boy's clothes and, aged thirteen, became a foot-page to 'a French lady'. Later she joined the Navy, moved on to the Army, fell in love with a soldier and married him.

The story might have ended there, but Mary's husband died and, for some reason, she joined a ship bound for the West Indies. On the way there the ship was attacked by pirates, led by John Rackham (known as 'Calico Jack') accompanied by his mistress, Anne Bonney. Mary was captured.

She is said to have settled happily enough into a life of piracy, eventually falling in love with one of their captives and even fighting a duel on his behalf.

When 'Calico Jack' and his gang were taken, and tried in St Jago de la Vega, Jamaica, Mary Read was among them. Rackham was executed, Anne Bonney reprieved. Mary, being pregnant, had her sentence delayed, but according to Daniel Defoe she fell ill of a fever in prison and died there.

MARTHA REAY

1742–1779 (or Ray)
Royal Opera House, Covent Garden, WC2

As the audience left the Opera in Covent Garden two shots rang out across the piazza and a woman fell to the ground. She was dead by the time a doctor arrived. A young man, still holding two pistols, was wounded but alive . . . the second shot, intended for himself, had misfired.

The woman, Martha Reay, was the mistress of Lord Sandwich and had borne him several children. For many years her life had been calm and uneventful. She had lacked nothing. Then a young Captain, James Hackman, fell passionately in love with her. Secretly they became lovers, but Martha's conscience troubled her. Thinking of her children's future and her loyalty to Lord Sandwich, she could not bring herself to leave them. James Hackman went away for two years, but, unable to forget her, returned and wrote:

My dearest Life!
I never think of you but with a pleasing pain, the consequence of that great love of which, I hope, I have given you every proof in my power. I never bring you to my recollection . . . but with inexpressible anxiety . . . while I know you are not wholly mine, so great is my misery, that I cannot express it . . .

He left the army, was ordained and, begging her to marry him, obtained a living in Norfolk. Lord Sandwich intervened and James was warned to leave her alone, but it was Martha who finally had to convince him. She was tired of him, she said, she had taken another lover, she said. She refused to see him.

It was then that the Reverend James Hackman decided to kill himself in her presence and sat one evening in a coffee house in Covent Garden, waiting for the audience to leave the Opera House.

Martha Reay was buried in the churchyard at Elstree; James Hackman was later tried and executed.

Martha Reay (Ray) is buried in Elstree Parish Churchyard

DOROTHY RICHARDSON

1873–1957
(Mrs Odle)
Lived: Endsleigh Street,
WC1

TO THE MEMORY OF
DOROTHY MIRIAM ODLE
AUTHORESS D. M. RICHARDSON
A PIONEER AMONG NOVELISTS,
17TH MAY 1873 - 17TH JUNE 1957.
THE WIDOW OF ALAN ODLE, ARTIST.

Dorothy Richardson went to school in Putney and when she was eighteen left home to take a post as a pupil-teacher in Germany. She returned to look after her mother, who was seriously depressed and who later committed suicide. Dorothy taught for a while at a school in North London. She then worked as secretary-assistant in a dental practice in Harley Street, moving to Bloomsbury (Endsleigh Street), where she studied, read, observed and began to write:

> London, just outside all the time, coming in with the light, coming in with the darkness, always present in the depths of the air in the room . . .

Dorothy Richardson's gravestone in Streatham Park Cemetery

Her novels, such as *Pointed Roofs* (1915) and *Backwater* (1916), anticipated the stream-of-consciousness technique of James Joyce and Virginia Woolf, but failed to gain for her the reputation she deserved. Her books are now being re-published.

She had an affair with H. G. Wells, moved to St John's Wood, and there met and married Alan Odle. They led an unobtrusive life. She is buried in Streatham Park Cemetery.

FRANCES, DUCHESS OF RICHMOND AND LENNOX

1647–1702
Effigy: Westminster
Abbey Museum

The Richmond and Lennox monument is in a small chapel off the Henry VII Chapel in Westminster Abbey. Frances Theresa was buried in the vault below.

She was considered a great beauty in her day and sat for the original figure of 'Britannia' used on the coinage until recently. Her effigy, dressed in the robes that she wore to Queen Anne's coronation, is in the Abbey museum. Beside it perches her favourite parrot, looking as if he wonders whether it is worth being one of the oldest stuffed birds in England.

Effigy of the Duchess of
Richmond and Lennox in
Westminster Abbey
Museum

ANNE ISABELLA RITCHIE

1837–1919
(née Thackeray)
Lived: 16 Young Street,
W8 and 36 Onslow
Square, SW7

For some years, William
Makepeace Thackeray's daughter
worked as his secretary. Her own
first appearance in print came in
1860, and she continued to write
for the rest of her life. In 1877, to a
chorus of disapproval, she married
her younger cousin, Richmond
Ritchie.

Anne's books are full of
delightful surprises. Her romantic
novel, *Miss Angel*, was based on
the life of the artist Angelica
Kauffmann (q.v.), but it was in her
essays and memoirs that she
excelled in her ability to bring
people vividly to life. Who, having

read it, could forget her description
of Charlotte Brontë's visit to the
Thackerays' home in Young Street,
Kensington?

> After a moment's delay the door
> opens wide, and the two gentlemen
> come in, leading a tiny, delicate,
> serious little lady, pale, with fair
> straight hair and steady eyes . . . she
> is dressed in a little barège dress
> with a pattern of faint green moss.
> She enters in mittens, in silence, in
> seriousness: our hearts are beating
> with wild excitement.

Anne Thackeray Ritchie was
buried, with her husband, in
Hampstead Cemetery.

MARY ROBINSON ('PERDITA')

1758–1800
(née Darby)
Portrait 'Perdita', by
Gainsborough, The
Wallace Collection,
Hertford House,
Manchester Square, W1

Mary's father, abroad on business,
left his family in Bristol. On his
return, having acquired a mistress,
he sold the house and moved the
family to London, placing the
children at school and his wife in
lodgings . . . Mr Darby then
departed.

When Mary's school closed, Mrs
Darby opened a small
establishment of her own. Her
husband, on a visit, was aghast at
the possible effect of this
commercial enterprise on his
reputation and soon put a stop to
such nonsense. He moved them to
different lodgings, sent Mary to
another school – and went away.

Mary became interested in
poetry and dancing. At fifteen she
was introduced to David Garrick,
who began to coach her for the
stage, but her mother, fearing the
disreputable theatre, pushed her
daughter into marriage with a Mr
Robinson. It was disastrous. Soon

pregnant, Mary was neglected by a
wastrel husband who ran into debt
and was sent to prison. After his
release she joined the theatre in
1776 and, appearing before the
royal family in 1779 as Perdita in
A Winter's Tale, enchanted the
Prince of Wales (later George IV).
Finally, overwhelmed by his
passionate pursuit, letters and
promises, Perdita, as he called her,
gave in. She moved to a suitable
house and for two years they were
'noticed' everywhere together.
Then George came of age. Perdita
was abandoned.

In debt, and without the
promised 'allowance' (although an
annuity was finally obtained for
her), Mary then became seriously
ill. A semi-invalid, she earned some
money by writing, but the rest of
her life was to be a struggle against
illness and poverty. Only
forty-two, she died at Englefield
and was buried in Old Windsor.

MARY ROGERS

d. 1899
Plaque: Postman's Park,
Aldersgate Street, EC1

The London and South Western
Railway Company's passenger
steamer, the *Stella*, left
Southampton on the morning of
30 March 1899, carrying about
140 passengers and a crew of forty.
At four o'clock that afternoon, in
dense fog, she struck rocks and
foundered. A large number of
those on board lost their lives. By 3
April *The Times* reported 102
people accounted for, out of a
possible 180.

Some of the survivors owed their
lives to a stewardess, Mary Rogers,
who:

. . . worked like a heroine tying
lifebelts on 'her' ladies, as she called
them, but apparently omitted one
for herself, for she is gone. (*The
Times* 3 April 1899)

She is remembered on a plaque
in what is known as 'Postman's
Park', once the churchyard of St
Botolph's, Aldersgate (near the
Museum of London), where, on an
arcade behind some benches, there
is a collection of tablets recording
acts of bravery by ordinary people.

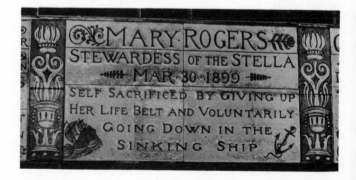

MARGARET ROPER

1505?–1544
(née More)
Crosby Hall, Chelsea,
SW3

Crosby Hall, Chelsea, the
home of Margaret Roper
and of her father, Sir
Thomas More

Daughter of Sir Thomas More
(Henry VIII's Lord Chancellor,
executed in 1534 for refusing to
take the Oath of Succession),
Margaret was born in the City of
London. After her mother's death,
and her father's second marriage,
the family moved to Chelsea.
Thomas More always had a special
affection for Margaret and
encouraged her intellectual ability,
which was much admired by
eminent scholars. Her translation
of *A Devout Treatise upon the
Paternoster* by Erasmus was
published in 1523. She married
William Roper and had five
children.

When her father, after his trial at
Westminster Hall, was being
returned to the Tower, Margaret
waited at Tower Wharf. Pushing
her way through the crowd to
receive his blessing, she then flung
her arms round his neck and kissed
him. In his last letter to her More
wrote: 'I never liked your manner
toward me better than when you
kissed me last.'

A copy of the painting of the
More family by Holbein hangs in
Crosby Hall, Chelsea, the site of
More's house. This is now the
college hall of the British
Federation of University Women,
who have named a study-bedroom
after Margaret.

CHRISTINA ROSSETTI

1830–1894

Plaque: 30 Torrington
Square, WC1

The daughter of Italian immigrants, Christina was born in London. She wrote poetry from an early age and her grandfather, proud of her ability, printed a small volume of her verse when she was seventeen. Her brother, Dante Gabriel Rossetti, sometimes used her as a model and she sat for his early Pre-Raphaelite painting *Girlhood of Mary Virgin* (now in the Tate Gallery). When he and his friends started their journal, *The Germ*, Christina contributed poems under the pseudonym of Ellen Alleyne. She continued to write a great deal of beautiful lyric poetry and her *Goblin Market and Other Poems* was published in 1862.

Her engagement to James Collinson, the artist, was broken off because of religious differences. She never married, but as she got older became more and more absorbed by the religious life. Christina was buried in the Rossetti family grave in Highgate Cemetery (West).

> When I am dead my dearest,
> Sing no sad songs for me;
> Plant thou no roses at my head,
> Nor shady cypress tree:
> Be the green grass above me
> With showers and dewdrops wet;
> And if thou wilt, remember,
> And if thou wilt, forget.

The Rossetti family grave
in Highgate Cemetery
West

MARIA RYE

1829–1903
Lincoln's Inn Fields area,
WC2

Interested in charitable work and convinced that women should be offered a wider range of opportunities, Maria Rye, with great energy, set out to improve the situation. Near Lincoln's Inn in London she ran a law-stationer's which offered employment to girls, then helped to establish the Victoria Printing Press as well as a registry office and telegraph school in Bloomsbury. In 1861, having successfully raised a fund for assisting middle-class girls to emigrate, she founded the Female Middle Class Emigration Society,

but from 1868 she concentrated on the emigration of pauper children.

The 'gutter children', as she called them, were trained at first in a home in Peckham and then taken to Canada, where their training continued at a similar home in Niagara. They were then found jobs as domestic servants. Maria herself accompanied each group to Canada, and once they were settled insisted on visiting them regularly. She retired to Hemel Hempstead in Hertfordshire where she died, and was buried in the churchyard there.

FLORA SANDES

1876–1955
(Mrs Yudenitch)
Imperial War Museum,
Lambeth Road, SE1

For a long time, when walking down the street, I had to clench my hand to keep from saluting mechanically . . . It was impossible, at first, to remember not to click the heels together when introduced to anyone. (*The Autobiography of a Woman Soldier*)

Flora Sandes, nearly forty when she volunteered as a nurse at the beginning of the 1914–18 war, was sent to Serbia as a member of an ambulance unit. She fell ill during a typhoid epidemic and went back to London to convalesce, but on her return volunteered for duty with the ambulance of the 2nd Serbian Infantry Regiment. Flora stayed with them, sharing their life, their hardships and eventually their battles, until she was accepted as a soldier and made a corporal. In 1916, fighting in Macedonia, she was severely wounded by a

grenade:

> The Serbs have a theory that you must not give water to a wounded man because they say it chills him, so they poured fully half a bottle of brandy down my throat instead, and put a cigarette in my mouth.

In hospital for almost six months, Flora was awarded the highest decoration a Serbian soldier could be given, the King George Star. She then returned to her regiment and was made a Sergeant-Major. When she retired, a commissioned officer, in 1922, and married Sergeant Yurie Yudenitch, she had been in the Serbian Army for seven years.

Flora settled in Yugoslavia with her husband, but after his death she went back to England where she lived in a cottage in Suffolk for the last ten years of her life.

MRS LORD GEORGE SANGER

1832–1899
(née Ellen Chapman)
Site of Agricultural Hall,
Upper Street, N1

Before her marriage to George Sanger, Ellen Chapman starred in Wombwell's Menagerie as 'Madame Pauline de Vere' – a glamorous and intrepid lion-tamer. (There were three rival 'Lion Queens' at the time, but one of them was killed by a tiger and all such performances by women were promptly banned.)

After their marriage, the young couple leased the bizarre Enon Chapel, near the Strand. Speculators, knowing that about twelve thousand bodies were

buried under the floor-boards, had bought the chapel, installed a brick floor, and turned it into a dance-hall: 'Enon Chapel – Dancing on the Dead – Admission three pence'.

The bodies had been removed and reburied when the Sangers took over and presented a pantomime there ('. . . Mrs Sanger skipped it on the light fantastic toe as Columbine . . .'). Unfortunately more bodies were discovered and their theatre was closed down. Undaunted, they travelled with their own circus-show so successfully that, by 1871, they were able to buy Astley's Amphitheatre in Westminster, and also lease the Agricultural Hall in Islington.

Ellen threw all her energy into helping her husband but she never forgot her lions and often appeared in processions as Britannia, her favourite lion lying at her feet. In

1875 Thomas Frost wrote:

> The Sangers possess lions at the present day, and one of them is so tame that, as I am informed, it is allowed to roam at large in their house, like a domestic tabby.

Ellen died in London but was buried in the Sanger family vault in Margate Cemetery.

DOROTHY L. SAYERS

**1893–1957
(Mrs Fleming)**
St Anne's Church Tower, Soho, W1 (not always open)

Dorothy L. Sayers was born in Oxford and later attended Somerville College there. Moving to London, she began to write detective stories and created her inimitable hero, Lord Peter Death Bredon Wimsey.

In 1926 she married the journalist Oswald Fleming. They moved to Witham, Essex, where Dorothy continued to write. *The Nine Tailors*, considered by many Sayers addicts to be her best thriller, was published in 1934. A novel with Oxford as a background, *Gaudy Night*, was published the following year.

Later she turned to religious themes, and her controversial play *The Man Born to Be King* based on the life of Christ, was serialised on radio. She also wrote poetry and translated Dante's *Inferno*. Her London home was 24 Great James Street, Bloomsbury, and, although she died at Witham, her ashes were placed in a chapel at the base of St Anne's Church tower in Soho.

DR MARY ANN SCHARLIEB, DBE

**1845–1930
(née Bird)**
Harley Street, W1

> My dearest Mrs Scharlieb
> This day, 29 December, is the anniversary of the saving of my life . . . you brought me back to life and work again in 1897 . . . (letter from Marie Corelli, 1901)

Mary Scharlieb received her licentiate in medicine, surgery and midwifery at Madras Medical College in 1878. She had lived in India for nearly thirteen years and had three children. When she returned to London, hoping to obtain an English degree, she encountered a certain lack of enthusiasm:

> I also had an introduction to Mr Bryant, Surgeon at Guy's Hospital. When I went to see him he said: 'Let us understand each other: I entirely disapprove of women becoming doctors and will do nothing to further your wishes.' However, after a careful explanation of the situation as I conceived it, he altered his opinion.

So Mrs Scharlieb entered the London School of Medicine for Women, took her MB in 1881 and two years later was studying operative midwifery in Vienna. On her return to India, she worked for a while as a GP, was then appointed non-resident Superintendent of the Royal Victoria Hospital for Caste and Gosha women and also became lecturer and examiner at Madras Medical College. Not surprisingly by the time she was in her early forties her health was suffering. She retired to London and a house in Harley Street.

After a while her 'retirement' merely renewed her energy and, by 1897, she had obtained the London MS degree and was lecturing in midwifery. When she was appointed gynaecologist to the Royal Free Hospital, she became the first woman to hold a staff appointment in a London general hospital. A ward at the Royal Free was named after her.

ELIZABETH SCOTT

1898–1972
(Mrs Richards)
Royal Institute of British Architects, 66 Portland Place, W1

Elizabeth Scott, FRIBA, who had attended the Architectural Association Schools and gained her diploma in 1924, won an international competition in 1928 for designing the new Shakespeare Memorial Theatre in Stratford-upon-Avon:

> Miss Elizabeth Scott, by winning, has produced the strongest argument against that section of the community which derides the idea that a woman may make a successful architect. (*Architects Journal*, January 1928)

The partnership of 'Scott, Chesterton and Shepherd' was then formed, consisting of Elizabeth, her previous employer, Maurice Chesterton, and her colleagues, Alison Sleigh and J. C. Shepherd. They worked later on the extensions to Newnham College, Cambridge. After her marriage Elizabeth gave up architectural practice. She was, for many years, a member of the Fawcett Society, in London.

HARRIET SHELLEY

1795?–1816
(née Westbrook)
The Serpentine, Hyde Park, SW1

Harriet first met Percy Bysshe Shelley while she was still at school in London, and, aged sixteen, eloped with him. They were married in Edinburgh. Whatever the reasons – their youth, Harriet's naïveté, Shelley's theories on free love – their relationship rapidly deteriorated, not even improving after the birth of their daughter.

Although Harriet was again pregnant, Shelley left England with Mary Godwin (see Mary Shelley) before the child was born in 1814.

Harriet lived for a while at her father's house. She sent the children to live in the country and, after a brief affair, she moved into lodgings in 1816. One evening she quietly left the house and drowned herself in the Serpentine lake in Hyde Park.

MARY SHELLEY

1797–1851
(née Godwin)
Plaque: 24 Chester Square, SW1

It was on a dreary night of November that I beheld the Accomplishment of my toils. With an anxiety that almost amounted to agony, I collected the instruments of life around me, that I might infuse a spark of being into the lifeless thing that lay at my feet.

And so, for the first time, Frankenstein's monster stirred and opened his 'dull yellow eyes'. Mary's first novel was begun after an evening spent with her husband (the poet Shelley) and Lord Byron at a villa on Lake Geneva. They had discussed ghosts and then Byron had suggested that they should each write a ghost story. Byron's and Shelley's efforts came to nothing, but Mary persisted and the result was *Frankenstein*, published in 1818.

Born in London, she was the daughter of Mary Wollstonecraft (q.v.) (who died after Mary's birth) and William Godwin. Even when

young her father noted that she was: 'somewhat imperious and active of mind'. At seventeen she ran off with Shelley and, after his wife's suicide in 1816, married him. They spent a great deal of time in Italy, but after her husband's tragic death by drowning, Mary settled in England, writing to earn her living. She wrote several novels and also edited two collections of Shelley's poems. Although she died in London, she was buried in Bournemouth.

CLARE SHERIDAN

1885–1970
(née Frewen)
Married: St Margaret's
Church, Westminster,
SW1

I envy those people who can simply get on with their jobs and are filled with confidence. The world seems less nonsensical to them.

Clare Sheridan once referred to herself as an 'instinctive anarchist', who resented discipline. Her cousin, Winston Churchill, described her as a revolutionary. In 1910, she married Frederick Sheridan and had two daughters. When the younger child died, Clare began to learn to model in clay and then to sculpt. Her husband was killed in the First World War, just after the birth of their son, and she moved into a studio near Regent's Park in London where she struggled to earn her living by sculpting. In 1920 she was invited to Russia, where she did portrait busts of some of the revolutionary leaders, including Lenin and Trotsky. When she returned to London she found that she was regarded with cold disapproval and shunned by many of her friends.

Clare went to America where she worked as a journalist and correspondent for the New York *World* and travelled extensively. She settled for a while with her children in Constantinople, wrote, continued to sculpt and often found herself at odds with current opinion. When she died, she was buried close to Brede church near her home at Brede, in Sussex. The last of her autobiographies, *To the Four Winds*, was published in 1957.

ELIZABETH SIDDAL

1829–1862
(Mrs Dante Gabriel
Rossetti)
Buried: Highgate
Cemetery (West), Swains
Lane, N6

The Rossetti family grave, in Highgate Cemetery (West), is battered and the inscriptions are becoming difficult to read. Christina, Dante Gabriel Rossetti's sister, (q.v.) is buried there, and so is Lizzie, his wife.

After a painfully long 'engagement', Rossetti had finally married her in 1860 and, the following year, she gave birth to a stillborn daughter. One evening in 1862 she took an overdose of laudanum and died the following morning. Distraught, Rossetti had the manuscript of his poems placed in her coffin and buried with her. Rossetti later repented his decision and the poems were removed from the grave.

Lizzie Siddal, born in London, had been 'discovered' working in a milliner's shop near Leicester Square by the artist Walter Deverell. He introduced her to his friends, and with her pale, fragile beauty and glorious red-gold hair, she became the model and inspiration for the group of painters who called themselves the Pre-Raphaelite Brotherhood. She modelled for Rossetti, for Holman Hunt and for Millais' painting *Ophelia* (Tate Gallery).

Rossetti and Lizzie were unofficially engaged and lovers from 1851, but he continually avoided the commitment of marriage. Lizzie became more and more unhappy and, never very strong, her health deteriorated rapidly. She started to draw and illustrate, with the encouragement of John Ruskin, the art critic, who taught her painting techniques and gave her an allowance. Later she began to write poetry, often stark and frighteningly intense:

> Turn thou away thy false dark eyes,
> Nor gaze upon my face;
> Great love I bore thee: now great hate
> Sits grimly in its place.

SARAH SIDDONS

**1775–1831
(née Kemble)**
Statue: St Mary's Church
gardens, Paddington
Green, W2

If you ask me 'What is a Queen?', I
should say – Mrs Siddons. (Tate
Wilkinson, 1790)

Born at the 'Shoulder of Mutton'
public house in Brecon, Wales,
Sarah became one of the greatest
tragic actresses in the history of the
British stage. Although not
everyone liked her, almost
everyone admired her and her
somewhat awesome respectability
was rarely challenged:

> Indeed she was always her own
> guard, and as was said of her later,
> one would as soon think of making
> love to the Archbishop of
> Canterbury.

She was buried at St Mary's
Church, Paddington Green, where
a statue of her sits in the gardens,
gazing over the nearby motorway.
A painting of her as the Tragic
Muse, on which the statue was
based, hangs in Dulwich College
picture gallery. When he had
finished it, Sir Joshua Reynolds
signed his name on the dress:

> I would not lose the honour this
> opportunity offered me of going
> down to posterity on the hem of
> your garment.

Two views of Sarah
Siddons: one looking out
over Harrow Road from
St Mary's Church
Gardens, Paddington
Green; the other tucked
away in Westminster
Abbey

DAME EDITH SITWELL

1887–1964

Lived: Pembridge Square area, W2

Born in Scarborough, Yorkshire, Edith Sitwell died in London and was buried at Weedon Lois in Northamptonshire. Her obituary in *The Times* was headed: 'Poetess of elaborate style and originality'.

She was also a woman of elaborate style and originality. Lonely as a child, and not at all beautiful by conventional standards, she cultivated an elegantly bizarre image throughout her life. Primarily a poet (*Gold Coast Customs* [1929], *Song of the Cold* [1945] and *Façade*, poems read to music especially composed by William Walton and first performed in 1923), she also wrote prose, including two studies of Elizabeth I, for whom she felt a great affinity – *Fanfare for Elizabeth* (1946) and *The Queen and the Hive* (1962). Her autobiography, *Taken Care Of*, was published posthumously in 1965.

Her standing as a poet and the debt she is owed by other, more recent, poets has not, even now, been fully appreciated.

DAME ETHEL SMYTH

1858–1944

Royal Albert Hall, Kensington Gore, SW7

Ethel was sent to a school in Putney in 1872, where, she said, she learned how to darn stockings and put clean linen at the bottom of a pile! Against strong parental opposition she achieved her desire to study music at Leipzig conservatory and stayed in Germany for eight years. On her return her 'Mass in D' had a great success at the Albert Hall, but was not performed again for another thirty-one years. Of her operas, *Der Wald* was well received in Germany and *The Wreckers* first performed in London in 1909.

Ethel became involved with the Women's Suffrage movement and adored Emmeline Pankhurst. They were both imprisoned at Holloway in 1913 where Ethel formed a choir of prisoners. She wrote the Suffragette anthem, *The March of Women*, became deaf in old age and died in Woking.

Inclined to emotional relationships with women, Ethel Smyth was engaged once (to Oscar Wilde's brother, Wilfrid) for three weeks. He proposed during a rough crossing of St George's Channel (Ethel was very sea-sick at the time).

HANNAH SNELL

1728–1792

Buried: Royal Hospital, Chelsea, SW3 (unmarked)

Born in Worcester, Hannah, as a child, took great delight in 'playing soldiers' with her friends. When she was seventeen, she moved to London, living there with her sister and, in 1743, married James Summs, a Dutch seaman. He soon abandoned her. Their child died, aged seven months, and Hannah, disguised as a young man, joined Captain Miller's company of Guise's Regiment of Foot. She then transferred to the navy, as an assistant steward and cook. During an engagement on land at Pondicherry, she was severely wounded, but the Indian woman who nursed her kept her sex a secret, and Hannah rejoined the navy, this time as a 'common sailor'. It was then that she is rather dubiously reported to have been put in irons for twelve days and given twelve lashes (having been wrongfully accused of stealing another sailor's shirt).

The whole adventure seems to have been an attempt to find her erring husband. When she heard that he was dead, she returned to dry land, petticoats, and London. Her biography was first published in 1750 and she also appeared at Sadlers Wells theatre, performing military exercises.

Hannah Snell married again, was allowed a military pension, and ran a pub called 'The Female Warrior', but, in 1789, she became insane and was sent to Bethlehem Hospital.

LADY HENRY SOMERSET

1851–1921
(née Isabel
Somers-Cocks)

I wonder if any one can understand how really mediocre I know myself to be?

Strictly brought up, and educated by a succession of governesses, Isabel married Lord Henry Somerset, the second son of the Duke of Beaufort, in 1872. The marriage was a failure, she was treated badly and the birth of a son did not improve matters. Encouraged by her strong-willed and protective mother, Isabel left her husband and went home with her baby. This caused a scandal, and although a legal separation was arranged, Lady Somerset found herself isolated and ostracised by society. She had broken the rules.

When her father died she inherited Eastnor Castle in Herefordshire. Moving there, she became more and more involved with the local Methodists, the problems of the poor and the evils of drink. Soon she was speaking at meetings all over the country and became a member of the British Women's Temperance Association. Later she became President and was invited to tour America and speak on the subject to the Women's Association there. She was a great success, but on her return to England Lady Somerset found herself unable to agree with extremists of the movement, who believed in Total Abstinence, enforced by law. In 1903 she gave up the presidency.

After this she concentrated on running a home for convicted women drunkards on her property at Duxhurst, Reigate, in Surrey, spending some of her time there and the rest at her flat in London.

MARY SOMERVILLE

1780–1872
(née Fairfax)
Bust: Royal Society, 6
Carlton House Terrace,
SW1 (not open to the
public)

As soon as our engagement was known I received a most impertinent letter from one of his sisters, who was unmarried, and younger than I, saying she 'hoped I would give up my foolish manner of life and studies, and make a respectable and useful wife to her brother'. I was extremely indignant.

Fortunately, William Somerville did not share his sister's views, and Mary continued her studies of mathematics and astronomy, publishing her *Physical Geography* in 1848. She corresponded with Herschel, the astronomer, encouraged the young Ada Lovelace (q.v.), and was honoured by the Royal Astronomical Society and the Royal Geographic Society for her work. Although they lived in London for many years, the Somervilles moved to Italy in an attempt to improve William's health.

Over ninety when she died in Naples, Mary had continued

working into old age and her daughter described her at this time:

Mathematics . . . delighted and amused her to the end. Her last occupations, continued to the actual day of her death, were the revision and completion of a treatise, which she had written years before, on the 'Theory of

Differences' (with diagrams exquisitely drawn) and the study of a book on Quaternions.

Somerville College, Oxford, was named after her and the bust that the Royal Society commissioned of her is still displayed at 6 Carlton House Terrace.

JOANNA SOUTHCOTT

1750–1814
Monument: St John's Wood Church gardens, NW8

Behold the time shall come, that
These TOKENS which I have told THEE
Shall come to pass, and the BRIDE Shall APPEAR, and SHE coming forth
Shall be SEEN, that now is WITHDRAWN from the EARTH

(2nd of *Esdras*, Chap 7th, Verse 26th: Part of the inscription on Joanna Southcott's monument)

A farmer's daughter from Devonshire, Joanna Southcott finally emerged as a religious zealot and a prophetess. Her prophecies were sealed up and dated, so that later they could be opened and examined. When she moved to London in 1802 her followers organised chapels and meeting-places for her. She also began to interpret dreams and issued certificates for the millenium . . . half-sheets of paper, signed by herself and sealed on the back.

Announcing that she would bring forth Shiloh, the second Christ, Joanna showed such convincing symptoms of

pregnancy in 1814 (at the age of sixty-four), that six out of nine doctors who examined her said that, had she been younger, they would have expected her to give birth. Her followers, in a state of great excitement, proclaimed the second coming. Gifts were showered on her, among them an expensive cradle, donated by a 'lady of fortune', which was exhibited at a cabinet-maker's in Aldersgate Street. Hundreds of people went to look at it.

In November of the same year, she told a Dr Richard Reece that she was dying and directed that her body should be opened four days after her death. Her instructions were carried out, and this time fifteen doctors signed a declaration saying that she had *not*, in fact, been pregnant. Joanna Southcott's funeral and burial took place, in great secrecy, at what was then Mary-le-Bone burying-ground. The tomb was later destroyed but, in the 1960s, a monument was erected to replace it.

EMMA SOYER

1813–1842
(née Jones)
Buried: Kensal Green
Cemetery, NW10

Emma Jones, born in London,
studied music '. . . in consequence
of the commendations of the
celebrated Weber'. Then her
step-father, Monsieur Simonau, a
Flemish artist, began to train her.
She revealed a distinct talent for
drawing and painting and became
a professional artist. A young
woman with a strong personality
and a dry sense of humour, she
once wrote an article called
'Fashionable Precepts for the
Ladies' in which she mocked the
attitudes of the society around her:

> To move and think as you feel
> inclined are offences that no polite
> person can with delicacy forgive . . .
> On any sudden alarm, either faint

or fall into hysterics . . .
Nothing is more common than
pretensions to science or classical
literature: therefore hold such
studies and their professors in
profound contempt . . .
You will then become a
fashionable lady, and, in the midst
of congratulation, will entirely
forget the sacrifice of truth and
nature by which you have acquired
this enviable distinction.

When the brilliant chef, Alexis
Benoit Soyer, wooed her:

> His proposals of marriage were
> accepted, but not without
> opposition from her step-father,
> Simonau, who would have had his
> pupil marry anybody rather than a
> *cook.*

However, in 1837, she became Madame Soyer and the same year her husband was appointed chef to the Reform Club in London. Emma continued to paint and began to receive critical acclaim. She became known as 'the English Murillo'.

In Paris many of her pictures were exhibited, and her reputation there stands higher than even in her native country. Her works are all said to have been marked by great vigour and breadth of light and shadow.

Then, when her husband was away, Emma, expecting their first child, was prematurely confined during a terrifying thunderstorm. She died the same night. The monument to her in Kensal Green Cemetery was erected by her husband. The medallion on it was taken from a portrait done by her step-father.

LADY HESTER STANHOPE

1776–1839
Lived: Montagu Square, W1

Hester's youth was disturbed and restless. After her mother died she was brought up by an eccentric father, at fourteen she moved to her grandmother's and then, in 1803, to the home of her uncle, William Pitt. Three years later, after Pitt's death, and having bought a house in Montagu Square:

She glittered angrily for a while in the society of London, then, having seen its true worth, left it for ever to become Queen of the Desert. (Edith Sitwell)

Accompanied only by her maid, a footman and her companion, Dr Meryon (who later wrote three volumes of memoirs), Hester Stanhope left England in 1810. After many adventures she finally settled in Djoun – a deserted monastery – on Mount Lebanon in Syria. Here she studied astrology, entertained visitors, befriended the Bedouin, upset British residents and died. She was buried in the garden there.

I am contented with the violence of my own character; it draws a line for me between friends and enemies.

MARIE STOPES

1880–1958
'Marie Stopes' House,
108 Whitfield Street, W1

Marie Stopes, BSc, was an authority on Palaeobotany (the study of fossil plants) for many years. Her interest in sex education and birth control originated in her experience of marriage. When she filed her nullity petition in 1914, she had been married for five years, to R. R. Gates, but was still a virgin.

In 1918 she remarried and published *Married Love*, a book that, sensationally in those days, attempted to discuss marital sex. In 1921 she and her second husband, H. Verdon Roe, founded the Mother's Clinic for Constructive Birth Control. Marie's books and clinic were often savagely criticised and, in 1923, although advised against it, she insisted on bringing an action for libel against Dr Halliday Sutherland who had attacked her work in a book. She lost her case but gained widespread publicity for her cause. In 1924

The Times refused to print an announcement of the birth of her son.

Marie Stopes was a difficult and obstinate woman, but the value of her pioneering work in the field of contraception is undeniable. Dr Fox, giving the address at her memorial service in 1958, struck a tactful note:

'It fell to her, what falls to few of us, to espouse a cause which was strange to most, and shocking to many, and to see it at last generally accepted without protest and widely adopted as a matter of practice.'

Although much of her life was spent in London, Marie requested that at her death she should be cremated and her ashes scattered on the sea at Portland Bill, Dorset.

LADY JANE STRACHEY

1840–1928
(née Grant)
Died: Gordon Square,
WC1

All her life Jane Strachey took a great interest in Indian affairs. Her father, Sir John Grant of Rothiemurchus, had served there, and she married Major-General (later Lieutenant-General) Sir Richard Strachey in Calcutta in 1859. After years of travelling between India and Britain, she finally settled in London, began to publish some of her writings and continued to have children (she gave birth to thirteen altogether, one of whom was Lytton Strachey).

Always a supporter of women's suffrage, she became President of the Women's Local Government Society and a member of the Committee of the National Union of Women's Suffrage Societies. She was also one of the original subscribers to Girton College, Cambridge. An indomitable figure, she lived to the age of eighty-eight and died at her home in Gordon Square, London.

AGNES STRICKLAND

1796–1874
Lived: Bedford Square,
WC1

Agnes Strickland's first published work was her *Monody Upon the Death of the Princess Charlotte of Wales* (1817). She also wrote for children, but it was while her sister Elizabeth was editing the *Court Magazine* that they both became interested in the biographies of English queens. They began to research and write their *Lives of the Queens of England*, most of the work being done in London. There, they had some difficulty gaining access to the State Paper Office, Agnes's first application (to Lord John Russell) being met, apparently, with 'an uncourteous repulse'.

Published with Agnes's name alone given as the author (Elizabeth was opposed to publicity), the final result was a great popular success and the *Lives* have been used as a source of research ever since. They discovered, and included, informal details and domestic 'gossip' in a subject where such frivolity had previously been neglected.

Agnes continued her interest in historical research (her *Letters of Mary Queen of Scots* was published in 1842/43), and also wrote a novel, *How Will It End?* She retired to Southwold, in Suffolk, was granted a pension from the civil list and was buried in the churchyard there.

VIOLETTE SZABO

1921–1945
(née Bushell)
Plaque: 18 Burnley Road,
Brixton, SW9

Born in Paris, of an English father and a French mother, Violette grew up fluent in both languages. The family moved to England, living in Brixton, London, and when she left school, Violette worked in a hairdresser's and then as a shop-assistant. When war broke out in 1939, she joined the Land Army, but soon returned to London, where she met Etienne Szabo, an officer of the French Foreign Legion. They were married at Aldershot and after a brief honeymoon Etienne left with his regiment for North Africa. Violette joined the Women's Auxiliary Territorial Service (ATS), but had to leave as she was expecting a baby. A daughter was born in 1942. Later the news arrived that her husband had been killed in the battle of El Alamein.

Violette Szabo was then interviewed by the Special Operations Executive (SOE), accepted and sent for training. Although she was arrested twice by the Germans on her first fact-finding mission in France, she was released and returned safely to London. However, during her second mission she was captured and interrogated at Limoges and then sent to a prison at Fresnes, near Paris. She was interrogated, and tortured, at Gestapo Headquarters in Paris. In August 1944, she was among prisoners deported to Germany and taken to the concentration camp at Ravensbruck. She was executed there a few months before the German surrender, and was posthumously awarded the George Cross.

MARY ANN TALBOT

1778–1808
Somerset House, Strand, WC2

Mary claimed that she was the 'natural' daughter of Lord Talbot. Her mother had died at her birth and she was brought up near Chester by a married sister. When Mary was about fourteen, her sister died and she was placed under the guardianship of a Mr Sucker, who avoided this rather tedious responsibility by introducing her to Captain Bowen of the 82nd Regiment of Foot. He took her to London and seduced her. The regiment was ordered abroad. Mary was taken on board ship disguised as 'John Taylor', the Captain's foot-page, and later persuaded to enrol as a drummer-boy. Then Captain Bowen was killed at the Siege of Valenciennes. Mary deserted and joined the Navy, as a cabin-boy. Severely wounded in the Battle of Brest on the 'Glorious First of June', she was discharged and made her way back to London.

There, still in her role as John Taylor, and penniless, she applied to Somerset House for a pension and her share of the prize-money. They sent her to a prize-agent who told her to come back later. Mary Talbot lost her temper. She created such an appalling scene and used such foul language that she was marched off to Bow Street, where she told an astonished magistrate the whole story. A subscription was hurriedly raised to tide her over until the pension was paid.

She made every effort to earn a living but her wound gave her trouble and two long spells in hospital reduced her to begging. Then one day a publisher of Paternoster Row, Mr Kirby, witnessing a coach accident, was so distressed by the plight of a shabbily dressed woman whose arm had been broken that he offered her work as a domestic servant. He later published her story: *The Life and Surprising Adventures of Mary Ann Talbot – As Related By Herself.*

ELLEN TERNAN

1839–1914
Lodged: Berners Street, W1

Many of Charles Dickens's biographers seem convinced that the women in his novels were more carefully drawn after Ellen Ternan became his mistress. The most quoted example is that of Bella Wilfer in *Our Mutual Friend*. Unfortunately Dickens concealed his love-life so successfully that Ellen remains an insubstantial figure.

In June 1858, Dickens and his wife formally separated. There had been gossip about his relationship with Ellen, and in the same month, having barely begun her career as an actress, she left the stage. Her last performance was in a play called *Out of Sight, Out of Mind*. Dickens provided her with a house in Peckham and left her £1,000 in his will. Later Ellen married the Reverend George Robinson, principal of the High School, Margate. She was buried at Southsea.

ELLEN TERRY

1847–1928

Plaque: 215 King's Road, SW3

Casket in St Paul's Church, Covent Garden, WC2

A naturally gifted actress, Ellen Terry was a delightful person, described by all who knew her in the most affectionate terms. Intelligent and very beautiful, she had a wonderful sense of humour and great generosity. At the peak of her career she was Henry Irving's leading lady at the Lyceum Theatre for nearly twenty years.

Ellen's friendships were lasting, her marriages failures. The first, to the artist George Watts, when he was forty-seven and she seventeen, was a painful disaster. Watts sent her home after ten weeks, with six pounds a week 'as long as she led a chaste life'.

Later Ellen lived happily for many years with Edward Godwin, by whom she had two children. After this relationship deteriorated, two marriages to actors also foundered. Her memoirs are fascinating and her four lectures on Shakespeare were published as a book.

Ellen Terry died at Tenterden, Kent.

LAURA THISTLE-THWAYTE

1829–1894
(née Bell)
Buried: Paddington
Cemetery, Willesden
Lane, NW6

Having begun her career as a shop assistant in Belfast, Laura Bell soon discovered a far more rewarding profession and moved to London. Here her beauty and outrageous sense of style earned her the title of the Queen of London whoredom and an extravagant reputation: after one night, it was said, she had been given £250,000 by a Nepalese Prince. In 1852, when she visited the opera, the audience rose to watch her leave!

Laura married a Captain Thistlethwayte (a strange man who fired his pistol at the ceiling to summon a servant), lived in Grosvenor Square and enthusiastically took up religion. Her style did not desert her; beautifully dressed and adorned with jewels she preached eloquently. In 1887 her husband shot himself instead of the ceiling and Laura moved to Hampstead, continuing her good works.

EDITH THOMPSON

1894–1923
Executed: Holloway
Prison, N7

**Edith Thompson was
imprisoned and executed
at Holloway Prison in
1923**

One of the last women to be hanged in Britain, Edith Thompson, who worked as a book-keeper in Aldersgate Street, London, was married to Percy Thompson, a shipping clerk. They became friendly with Frederick Bywaters, a ship's clerk on the SS *Morea*, and in 1921 the three of them went on holiday together to the Isle of Wight. Edith and Frederick began an affair. Later he left their house in Ilford after a violent quarrel with Percy, and returned to his ship. He and Edith corresponded secretly – she destroyed his letters, but Frederick kept hers.

Late one October evening in 1922, Edith and her husband were walking home when Frederick appeared. After some angry words he stabbed Percy and ran off. Percy Thompson died of his wounds. Both Edith and Frederick were tried for murder at the Old Bailey in December 1922. Her letters were the main evidence against them. Full of fantasies and discussions about romantic novels, they seemed to hint that Edith wanted to get rid of her husband and were offered by the prosecution as clear intent.

The lack of letters from Frederick to Edith was brushed aside (later, when her mother asked how she could write 'such letters', Edith replied 'No one knows what kind of letters he was writing to me'). They were both found guilty and condemned to death. Edith's last words in court were, 'I am not guilty; oh, God, I am not guilty.' The appeal dismissed, Edith Thompson was executed at Holloway Prison in January 1923, Frederick Bywaters at Pentonville on the same day.

148

HESTER THRALE

**1741–1821
(later Piozzi)
(née Salisbury)**
The Anchor Pub ('Mrs
Thrale's bar'), Bankside,
SE1

Bored, and never wildly
enthusiastic about her husband,
Hester Thrale passed the time by
writing poetry and having
children. The Thrales either lived
in their home near Tooting, which
was then 'country', or in their
town house at Southwark, near her
husband's brewery. Dr Samuel
Johnson became a regular visitor
and encouraged Hester to write
more. Henry Thrale bought her a
set of calf-bound books, each one
stamped 'Thraliana', and in 1776
she began a diary. She
corresponded with Dr Johnson for
many years and their friendship
actually led to her being
commemorated on the side of his
statue (erected in 1910) behind St

Clement Dane's church in London.
However, when her husband
died and Hester married the singer
Gabriele Piozzi, not only did most
of her family and friends
disapprove, but Dr Johnson was
decidedly put out. Hester Piozzi
merely seemed remarkably happy,
until her second husband died in
1809. She then ended her diary:

> Everything most dreaded has
> ensued, – all is over; and my second
> husband's Death is the last Thing
> recorded in my first husband's
> Present! Cruel Death!

Originally from Wales, when she
herself died she was buried in
Tremeirchion Church in the Vale
of Clwyd.

FANNY TROLLOPE

**1780–1863
(née Milton)**
Lived Keppel Street, WC1

'. . . of all people I have known she
was the most joyous or, at any
rate, the most capable of joy.' So
wrote her son Anthony – perhaps,
of all her children, the one who
understood her best and the one
she understood least.

In 1827, hoping to improve the
dwindling family fortunes (and
also, one can't help feeling, for the
sheer hell of it) Fanny set off for
America.

> On the 4th of November . . . I sailed
> from London, accompanied by my
> son and two daughters; and after a
> favourable, though somewhat
> tedious voyage, arrived on
> Christmas-day at the mouth of the
> Mississippi.

She was forty-seven and had left
her husband – and son Anthony –
at home in England. Although she
stayed for three years, Fanny did
not enjoy the experience. America,
on the whole, left her cold, and
when she returned to London she

distilled her opinions, adventures
and observations into a book, *The
Domestic Manners of the
Americans*, in two volumes. In
Britain her caustic wit and racy
style made it a best-seller.

> The ladies have strange ways of
> adding to their charms. They
> powder themselves immoderately,
> face, neck and arms, with
> pulverised starch; the effect is
> indescribably disagreeable by
> day-light, and not very favourable
> at any time.

The Americans, understandably,
were not amused. Fanny never
quite achieved the same success
again, although by the time she
was seventy-six she had produced
114 volumes. She supported her
family financially, nursed them
through tragic illnesses, continued
to travel and died, in Florence,
aged eighty-three. She was buried
in the English cemetery there.

MARY TUDOR (QUEEN)

1516–1558
Buried: Westminster
Abbey

The daughter of Henry VIII and his
divorced first wife, Catherine of
Aragon, Mary spent most of her
youth in isolation, declared
illegitimate and clinging
desperately to her mother's devout
Catholicism. As a result, when she
became Queen in 1553, she not
only attempted to reverse the
upsurge of Protestantism, with

terrible consequences, but insisted
on marrying Philip of Spain against
all advice.

A pregnancy turned out to be
false, Philip left for Spain and
Mary died, a tragic, embittered
woman. She has never lost the title
of 'Bloody Mary', and is buried
with her half-sister, Elizabeth I
(q.v.), in Westminster Abbey.

ANNA MARIE TUSSAUD

1761–1850
(née Grossholtz)
Buried: St Mary's
Catholic Church,
Draycott Terrace, SW3

Having travelled extensively
throughout the British Isles since
1802, Madame Tussaud's
Waxworks Exhibition finally came
to rest in Baker Street, London, in
1835. Forty-nine years later it
moved into new premises just
round the corner in the
Marylebone Road. Today,
'Madame Tussaud's' is one of
London's most popular tourist
attractions.

Madame Tussauds,
Marylebone Road, NW1

The woman who founded it first
learned the art of modelling in wax
from her uncle, Dr Curtius, who
lived and worked in Paris under
the patronage of the Prince de
Conti. By the time she was
seventeen, Anna Marie was being
allowed to take casts and model
from life. When she was nineteen
she was appointed to teach
wax-modelling to Madame
Elizabeth, sister of the King (Louis
XVI). Anna Marie moved into the
palace at Versailles and lived there
for nine years. Just before the
Revolution erupted in 1789 she
returned to her uncle's home.

Dr Curtius and his niece
survived. They modelled heads of
the leaders of the revolution, and
during the 'Terror' Anna Marie is
said to have been forced to model
the head of the Princesse de
Lamballe (whom she had known at
Versailles) just after her brutal
murder by the crowd. She also had
to make a death-mask of the
Queen, Marie-Antoinette, after her
execution, which is still exhibited
at Madame Tussaud's.

Then Dr Curtius died. Anna
Marie sorted out a chaotic
inheritance and decided not only to
continue her uncle's exhibition,
but also to make additions to it. In
1795 she married François
Tussaud. They lived in Paris and
had two sons.

In 1802 Madame Tussaud took
part of her exhibition to Britain,
accompanied by one of her sons
and began to tour it all over the
country. When it opened
permanently in London she lived
close by, at 58 Baker Street.

'VESTA TILLEY'

1864–1952
(Lady de Frece)
(née Matilda Powles)
Green Park, Piccadilly,
W1

In 1869 a small girl called Matilda
appeared on stage as 'the pocket
Sims Reeves' (a famous tenor). She
had begun her career as a male
impersonator. Later, known as
'Vesta Tilley', audiences in London
flocked to see her as the smooth
'young man about town'. They
admired not only the performance
but her immaculate wardrobe as
'Burlington Bertie', 'Monty from

Monte Carlo' or, her own
favourite, 'Algy':

> He's very well-known is Algy –
> As the Piccadilly Johnny with the
>   little glass eye.

Married in 1890 to the
impresario Walter de Frece, she
retired when he was knighted in
1919. A ladder of violets decorated
the stage of the Coliseum for her

farewell performance and she was given seventeen curtain calls. Later they lived for many years in the South of France, but after her husband's death Vesta Tilley returned to London. She died in her flat overlooking Green Park.

LOUISA TWINING

1820–1912
St Clement Dane's,
Strand, WC2

In the years 1847 and 1848 my attention had been called to the condition of the poor, perhaps owing to heavy losses and trials in our family circle, and I first began to visit them in the old parish of St Clement Dane's, in the Strand, in which we were born.

Today, the fear of 'ending up in the workhouse' has almost been forgotten; in Louisa Twining's day, the fear was very real.

> The sick in the so-called infirmary, a miserable building, long since destroyed, were indeed a sad sight, with their wretched pauper nurses in black caps and workhouse dress. One poor young man was there, who had lain on a miserable flock bed for fourteen years with a spine complaint, was blind, and his case would have moved a heart of stone; yet no alleviation of food or comforts were ever granted him, his sole consolation being the visits of a good woman, an inmate, who had been a ratepayer, and attended upon him daily, reading to him while away the dreary hours.

The conditions were appalling, and as a result of her visits Miss Twining became a crusading reformer. She investigated, agitated, wrote pamphlets, letters, organised petitions, opened a home in London for ex-workhouse girls and became a member of the Kensington Board of Guardians.

Louisa Twining published her memoirs, *Recollections of Life and Work*, in 1893, retired to Tunbridge Wells and died an unsung heroine.

MADAME LUCY VESTRIS

d. 1856
(née Bartolozzi)
Buried: Kensal Green
Cemetery, NW10

> 'Tis circumstance dignifies places;
> A desert is charming with Spring!
> And pleasure finds twenty new graces,
> Wherever the Vestris may sing.

In 1813, Lucy married Armand Vestris, a French dancer, at St Martin-in-the-Fields in London. She then became well-known as a delightful singer, actress and dancer. Widowed in 1825, six years later she opened the Olympic Theatre as sole lessee, and thus became the first 'actress-manageress' in London, much admired for the natural style of her direction and also for the reforms she initiated regarding the pay and conditions of her company. Her business sense, however, was weak, and she was later declared bankrupt, in spite of enormous popular success.

With her second husband, Charles Mathews, an actor, she toured America. On their return they managed Covent Garden Theatre for a few years, but overspent on lavish productions and had to give up at the end of their third season. In 1847 they opened the English Opera House, in Wellington Street, as the Lyceum Theatre and presented the kind of extravaganzas and comedies that had made Lucy's reign at the Olympic so popular, but just as success seemed assured, Lucy's health began to fail; she made her last appearance on stage in 1854 and spent her last two years confined to her room at home.

QUEEN VICTORIA

1819–1901
Statue: The Broad Walk,
Kensington Gardens, W8

At only eighteen, Queen Victoria ascended the throne in 1837. Three years later she married Albert of Saxe-Coburg-Gotha, whom she adored and (not at all amused by the process) gave birth to nine children. A widow for almost forty years, when she died, as Lytton Strachey later wrote: '. . . the vast majority of her subjects had never known a time when Queen Victoria had not been reigning over them.' Six children, forty grandchildren and thirty great-grandchildren survived her. She was buried at Frogmore, Windsor.

There are statues, memorials and reminders of Queen Victoria all over London. A statue in Kensington Gardens, near Kensington Palace, was the work of her daughter, Princess Louise.

BARBARA VILLIERS

**1641–1709
(Countess of
Castlemaine and
Duchess of Cleveland)**
Walpole House, Chiswick
Mall, W4 (No visitors)

Barbara Villiers' ghost is said to
haunt Walpole House, where she
spent her last years. Born in
London, she married Roger Palmer
when she was eighteen, but
continued an affair with Lord
Chesterfield. She probably met
Charles II in Holland, before the
Restoration, and wasted little time
before becoming his mistress.
Beautiful, ambitious and arrogant,
she was not very popular at court
but influenced the King for many
years. When she gave birth to a
daughter in 1661 Barbara claimed
it was the King's child and,
although there was some doubt,
persevered until Charles
acknowledged paternity thirteen
years later. A title was bestowed on
her husband so that Barbara could

also enjoy the privilege of rank.
   After his marriage to Catherine
of Braganza, the King insisted that
his wife should receive his mistress,
causing, naturally enough, the
most frightful quarrels. However,
although Barbara managed to
retain her influence for some time,
the attractive Frances Stuart
arrived at court and took her place.
   Barbara Villiers eventually
began to take other, often
disreputable, lovers and, aged
sixty-four, married a notorious
rake, only to discover a few
months later that he was already
married. She was given a
magnificent funeral and was buried
at St Nicholas's church, Chiswick.
There is no monument.

HELEN WADDELL
1889–1965
Lived: Primrose Hill Road, NW3

A brilliantly-gifted scholar and sensitive translator, Helen Waddell was born in Tokyo, educated at Victoria College and Queen's University, Belfast, and from 1920 to 1922 was a member of Somerville College, Oxford.

In 1927 she published *The Wandering Scholars* which included translations from the *Carmina Burana*, a collection of songs, some highly spiritual, others distinctly earthy, written in the twelfth and thirteenth centuries. Her name became known to a wider public when she published an historical novel, *Peter Abelard*, based on the tragic love story of the twelfth-century lovers, Heloïse and Abelard.

Helen Waddell lived in London for many years and bought a large, exhaustingly impractical house in Primrose Hill Road. When she died she was buried in Ireland.

Among those who have opened our eyes to the dawning romanticism and the humanism of the early Middle Ages Helen Waddell stood out for the grace of her learning, her love of fine literature and her poet's gift of translation. (Obituary in *The Times*, 1965)

PRINCESS CHARLOTTE OF WALES
1796–1817
St George's Chapel, Windsor, Berkshire

Mourn, Britain's Prince, thine only child is flown,
The fairest brilliant that adorned thy crown . . .

Charlotte was born at Carlton House, off the Mall, of which nothing survives except some columns incorporated into the façade of the National Gallery. She was the only child of those bizarre parents, George, Prince of Wales (later George IV) and Caroline of Brunswick, who separated six months after her birth. Against all odds she developed into a bouncy, independent and cheerfully eccentric young woman, the great hope of the British public, who were totally disillusioned by the rest of the royal family.

Charlotte married Prince Leopold of Saxe-Coburg in 1816 and then moved to Claremont (at Esher). In November 1817, having given birth to a still-born son, she died, aged twenty-one, and was buried at Windsor. There is an exceptionally moving and beautiful monument to her there, in a corner of St George's chapel.

NELLIE WALLACE
1870–1948
(Mrs Eleanor Jane Liddy)
Vaudeville Theatre, Strand, WC2

Born in Glasgow, Nellie began her career as a clog-dancer and then toured the music-halls as one of the 'Three Sisters Wallace'. She appeared in London for the first time in 1903 and soon established herself as one of the great comediennes of the British stage. She played the wicked witch Carabosse in *The Sleeping Beauty* at the Vaudeville Theatre and became one of the first – of very few – female Pantomime dames. Her act was later to earn her descriptions such as 'Mistress of

the Grotesque' and 'the essence of eccentricity'.

Before she died, she had been touring with Don Ross's *Thanks for the Memory*, and her last appearance on stage was in the Royal Variety Performance, 1948. She was cremated at Golders Green.

CATHERINE WALTERS

1839–1920
Plaque: 15 South Street,
W1

The pretty 'horse-breakers' ride in
the row,
And cause crowds to assemble
wherever they go.
But the one who is easily Queen of
them all,
Is dainty Miss Skittles, who holds us
in thrall.

On a house in South Street,
Mayfair, a blue plaque informs the
passer-by that 'Catherine Walters
(Skittles) the Last Victorian
Courtesan' lived there between
1872 and 1920. Her nickname and
her origins became confused by
colourful rumours, but 'Skittles'
certainly took London by storm.
She dazzled society with her
display of brilliant and daring
horsemanship when riding in Hyde
Park. She captivated Lord
Hartington and is thought to have
introduced the fashionable
'pork-pie' hat.

Her figure was exquisite, her
language notorious. It is said that
the Master of a fox hunt once
complimented her on her rosy
cheeks at the end of a chase.
'That's nothing,' came the reply,
'You should see my arse!'

Among her many, often
life-long, friends was the poet
Wilfrid Scawen Blunt. When she
died, known in respectable old age
as 'Mrs Bailey', it was he who
arranged her burial in the
churchyard of the Franciscan
Monastery at Crawley.

HORATIA NELSON WARD

1801–1881
(née 'Thompson')
Buried: Paine's Lane Cemetery, Pinner, Middlesex

My dear Horatia,
   I send you twelve books of Spanish dresses, which you will let your guardian angel, Lady Hamilton, keep for you when you are tired of looking at them. I am very glad to hear that you are perfectly recovered, and that you are a very good child. I beg, my dear Horatia, that you will always continue so; which will be a great comfort to your most affectionate
                    Nelson and Brontë

Horatia, the daughter of Emma, Lady Hamilton (q.v.) and her lover Lord Nelson, was born in London. To avoid scandal she was almost immediately transferred to a temporary foster-mother as the illegitimate child of an imaginary sailor, called 'Thompson', and in 1803 was baptised at Marylebone church. She was four years old, and living with Emma at Merton

as their 'adopted' daughter when Nelson died at Trafalgar. Almost his last words were:

> Remember, that I leave Lady Hamilton and my daughter Horatia as a legacy to my country – and never forget Horatia.

In 1812, when Emma was in financial difficulties, she fled to France, taking her daughter with her. Horatia, aged fourteen, was with her mother when she died. Brought up in England by her father's relatives, she later married the Reverend Philip Ward.
   Her parentage was, and remained for many years, painfully controversial: on her gravestone the inscription 'the *adopted* daughter of' was finally altered to read 'the *beloved* daughter of . . . Vice-Admiral Lord Nelson'.

MARY AUGUSTA WARD

1851–1920
(née Arnold)
Lived: Russell Square, WC1

Mary Arnold was born in Hobart, Tasmania, but the family returned to England and settled in Oxford when she was five. In 1872 she married Thomas Humphry Ward, moving to London when he joined the staff of *The Times* in 1881.
   Mrs Humphry Ward wrote several novels, the best known of which is *Robert Elsmere* (1888). She also founded the Women's National Anti-Suffrage League and helped to found the Passmore Edwards Settlement in Tavistock Square. It was there, in 1909, that

she took on Millicent Garrett Fawcett in a public debate on Women's Suffrage – losing heavily by 235 votes to 74.
   'I shall *never* do this sort of thing again, *never*,' she exclaimed afterwards, 'and I shall write to the papers to say so.' She was buried at Alderley, Herts, where she had lived for a time.

BEATRICE WEBB

1863–1943
(née Potter)
Plaque: 10 Netherhall Gardens, NW3

One of nine sisters, and the daughter of the President of the Great Trunk Railway in Canada and the Great Western Railway in England, Beatrice was presented at court when she was eighteen. In her twenties she began to investigate sweated labour in the East End of London, working as a 'trouser hand' to obtain first-hand knowledge about conditions there. In this way she was able to contribute towards Charles Booth's study, *Life and Labour in London*. She also became a socialist and a dedicated champion of the under-privileged.

Later, while making a study of the Co-operative Movement, she was introduced to Sidney Webb, a member of the Fabian Society:

> She had a mind of vivid observation and flashes of insight; she had learnt by conversation and discussion; but she was not really educated and trained. Webb was by nature a student, with enormous powers of assimilation, correlation and retention . . . He wrote steadily, convincingly, in an invariably round hand, and when he got to the goal there she was – descending, from her incredible broomstick . . .
> (H. G. Wells)

They married in 1892 and spent most of their honeymoon investigating the Trades Unions in Dublin. And so began the famous 'partnership of Webb and Webb', as they became affectionately known. Works by the Webbs include *The History of Trade Unionism* (1894), *The History of Local Government in England* (1929) and *Soviet Communism: A New Civilisation* (1936). When Sidney was elected Secretary for the Dominions and Colonies and then made first Baron of Passfield, Beatrice objected to being Lady Passfield and insisted on remaining plain 'Mrs Webb'.

In 1947 their ashes were placed in Westminster Abbey.

LONG MEG OF WESTMINSTER

c. 1530
Westminster Abbey Cloisters

I, Long Meg, once the wonder of the spinsters
Was laid, as was my right, i' the best of Minsters . . .

According to legend, the large black stone in the south walk of Westminster Abbey cloisters covered the remains of Meg, a notorious 'bawd' or brothel-owner during the reign of Henry VIII. At a much later date Dean Stanley ruined the legend by discovering that twenty-six monks, all victims of the plague, had actually been buried there.

Meg was, nevertheless, very successful during her lifetime and, in 1608, William Vaughan in *The Golden Grove* described one of her business techniques:

> . . . Some bawds have a dozen damsels, some lesse, yet of every man they take largely, as 20 shillings a weeke, or tenne pounds a month. It is said that Long Meg of Westminster kept alwaies 20 courtizans in her house, who by their pictures she sold to all commers.

AGGIE (AGNES) WESTON

1840–1918
Born: Bloomsbury area

It may seem to some that I ought to have been born within sound of the boatswain's whistle . . . but it was not so. Dear, smokey old London was my birthplace.

But Aggie, or 'Mother' Weston, as she became known, spent most of her life near the sea, closely involved with the lives and problems of the men who used her 'Sailor's Rest' homes. Inspired by her work for the Temperance Society, she and her friend Sophia Wintz opened the first home in Devonport in 1876 and five years later another in Portsmouth. Her sense of humour, undaunted energy and the help she gave to those in need later earned her this tribute from some sailors:

> We've named a gun after her, the 'Agnes Weston', and don't she speak out; and when she speaks

there's not many that can stand up against her.

A dedicated Christian, she summed up her achievements with these words: 'Of my whole life I

can truly say, "God's hand has been upon the tiller".' She died in Devonport and was buried there with full naval honours.

ELLEN WILKINSON
1891–1947
Palace of Westminster (Houses of Parliament), SW1

A slight gasp of polite astonishment greeted the appearance of Miss Wilkinson, the Labour Lady, in a vivid green dress. (*Daily Telegraph*, 1925)

No more than five feet tall, a red-head and a left-wing socialist, Ellen Wilkinson was nicknamed 'Red Ellen' or 'The Fiery Particle'. Manchester born, she stormed her way through elementary and secondary school on scholarships, and then took her MA at Manchester University. Teaching, she found, was too tame for her and in 1912 she joined the Independent Labour Party. After a brief flirtation with Communism, she was elected to Parliament as Labour candidate for Middlesbrough East in 1924, a seat she held for seven years.

Later, as the member for Jarrow, she led the Jarrow marchers in 1936 and also wrote an account of the tragedy of unemployment in Jarrow, *The Town that Was Murdered*. During the Second World War she was appointed as Parliamentary Secretary to the Ministry of Home Security:

> Often during the worst nights of the blitz Ellen was to be found in the middle of it, cheering the people in the shelters, moving about all over the place from the church crypts to the pubs – where I have seen her sink her pint with the firefighters during a break. (Ian Mackay in the *News Chronicle*, 7 February 1947).

She died in London, aged fifty-five, two years after she had been made Minister of Education.

ELLEN WILLMOTT
1858–1934
Brentwood Cathedral, Brentwood, Essex

The daughter of a London solicitor, Ellen was a talented amateur musician and photographer but also inherited a passion for gardening. When the family home, Warley Place in Essex, was left to her, she lavished a great deal of time, money and love expanding the garden there.

One of the first women Fellows of the Linnaean Society, she wrote an important monograph 'The Genus Rosa', and many plants were named both by her and for her. In 1920 she was asked to advise on the planting of Ann Hathaway's cottage-garden at Stratford-upon-Avon.

HARRIETTE WILSON
Died –c. 1846?
Lived for a while at 16 Trevor Square, SW7

Sir Walter Scott described her as '. . . a smart, saucy girl, with good eyes and the manners of a wild schoolboy'. Born in London, Harriette became the mistress of Lord Craven when she was only fifteen. An impressive procession of lovers, including the Duke of Beaufort and the Duke of Argyll, followed this youthful initiation. When she actually fell in love, the experience was to prove a disillusionment. 'Happiness,' she was to say later, 'is a stupid subject to write upon.'

When the Duke of Beaufort's son became involved with her, the Duke is said to have bribed her to go away and live in Paris, offering

her an annuity of £500 to do so. He then tried to pay her off with a lump sum of £1,200. Harriette, insulted, furious – and living in Paris – proceeded to write her memoirs, in four volumes, mentioning her lovers by name. She began, and continued, in defiantly impudent vein:

> I shall not say why and how I became, at the age of fifteen, the mistress of the Earl of Craven. Whether it was love, or the severity of my father, the depravity of my own heart, or the winning arts of the noble lord . . . does not now signify; or if it does, I am not in the humour to gratify curiosity in this matter.

The day each volume was due, people mobbed the publishers (Stockdale's of Covent Garden) and barriers were erected to control the crowds. Harriette Wilson had made her point, and when she threatened to publish further instalments her ex-lovers are said to have clubbed together to buy her off. She eventually married a Monsieur Rochfort and died a respectable widow!

PEG WOFFINGTON

1715–1760
Buried: St Mary with St Alban (Teddington Parish Church), Teddington, Middlesex

Peg's most popular role was as Sir Harry Wildair in *The Constant Couple*. She specialised in what were known as 'breeches' parts and in Dublin, where she was born, they sang:

> That excellent Peg!
> Who showed such a leg
> When lately she dressed in man's
>   clothes,
> A creature uncommon
> Who's both man and woman,
> And the chief of the belles and the
>   beaux!

A great success in London and much admired as a comedy actress, Peg was also credited with a hectic love life. She is said to have remarked to a friend that she had played Sir Harry so often that half the town believed her to be a man. 'Madam,' came the reply, 'the other half *knows* you to be a woman!' For a while she lived with, and nearly married, David Garrick.

When Peg's popularity waned she tried tragedy, but her voice was not suitable. She lived with her sister in a house in Teddington where a cottage tea-room in the High Street is named after her.

Peg Woffington's cottage is now a tea-room in Teddington

MARY WOLL-STONECRAFT

1759–1797
First Burial: Old St Pancras Churchyard, NW1

Wollstonecraft's body was moved from London to Bournemouth in 1851 but the headstone of her original grave still stands in the gardens of Old St Pancras churchyard. On it, after her name, come the words, 'Author of a Vindication of the Rights of Women' and, although she wrote much else, this book (published in 1792) became her best-known work. It was a battle-cry.

Mary, born in London, was tormented all her life by a brilliant mind and a restless, uncompromising spirit. She taught,

wrote, visited Paris during the Revolution, took a lover there and gave birth to a baby daughter, Fanny. Deserted, she attempted suicide in her despair, but then met and lived with William Godwin. In 1797 she married him but died after the birth of their child [see Mary Shelley].

Mary Wollstonecraft's memorial in the gardens of Old St Pancras Churchyard, NW1

ELLEN (MRS HENRY) WOOD

1814–1887
(née Price)
Buried: Highgate
Cemetery (West), Swains
Lane, N6

Novelist and later proprietor of *Argosy* magazine, Ellen suffered from curvature of the spine and often wrote in a reclining chair, the manuscript supported on her knees. Her immensely popular novel, *East Lynne*, was dramatised and a line, often quoted – 'Dead! And never called me mother!' –

gives a feeling of its emotional climax – though it was not in the book!

Born in Worcester, she lived in London after her marriage and was buried in Highgate Cemetery (West). The impressive tomb was copied from that of Scipio Africanus in Rome.

VIRGINIA WOOLF

1882–1941
(née Stephen)
Plaque: 29 Fitzroy
Square, W1

Virginia Woolf was born at 22 Hyde Park Gate, SW7

Hers was a work more of radiance than of fire. (Edith Sitwell)

Virginia Stephen was born at 22 Hyde Park Gate, Kensington. A plaque in Fitzroy Square marks one of her several homes in the Bloomsbury area. She married Leonard Woolf in 1912 and three years later they moved to Hogarth House, Paradise Road, in Richmond, Surrey, where they founded the Hogarth Press.

Virginia Woolfs first novel of importance, *Mrs Dalloway*, was published in 1925, then, among others, came *To The Lighthouse* (1927) and *The Waves* (1931). She also worked as a critic for the *Times Literary Supplement* and other journals.

The Woolf's had bought Monks House, Rodmell, Sussex, in 1919 as a country retreat and it was there that Virginia eventually gave up her long, unequal struggle against depression and was found, with stones in her pocket, drowned in the River Ouse. Her ashes were buried at the base of an elm tree in the garden there.

Hogarth House, Richmond, where Virginia and Leonard Woolf founded the Hogarth Press

HANNAH WOOLLEY

1623–168?
Old Bailey, EC4

Orphaned at fourteen, Hannah started a small school a few years later and then became a governess in a 'noble' household. After her marriage to Mr Woolley, they moved to London and established a boarding school for boys, where Hannah took on the role of matron and also produced four sons. She started to write recipe books after her husband's death, remarried, was widowed again and then published:

The Gentlewoman's Companion: A Universal Companion and Guide to the Female Sex in all Relations, Companies, Conditions and States of Life, even from Childhood down to Old Age; from the Lady at the Court, to the Cook-maid in the Country.

In 1674 she was living in the neighbourhood of the Old Bailey, but the date of her death and place of burial are unknown.

MARY ANN YATES

d. 1787
(née Graham)
Buried: St Mary's Church, Richmond, Surrey

Mrs Yates was one of that galaxy of talented actresses who dazzled London theatre audiences in the eighteenth century. Her first known appearance was as Marcia in Crisp's *Virginia* at Drury Lane. This was also her first appearance with David Garrick. She married Richard Yates, a comic actor, and they often worked together but in 1767 she moved to Covent Garden where she began to take on more tragic roles.

After her death her reputation as a fine actress earned her over three pages of unstinted praise in the *Gentleman's Magazine* of 1787. The eulogy by Francis Brooke ends:

Such *was* Mrs Yates; and, as memory can yet authenticate all that has been said, the publick will witness to its truth: her friends will say it falls below truth, and speaks the timid reserve of affection. May the remembrance of what she *was*, inspire emulation in the bosom of rising genius! And may it be said of some future votary of the dramatic muse, 'She rivals, she reminds us of Mrs Yates!'

AREA-BY-AREA GUIDE

In looking for different women's memorials, houses, etc. you will no longer be able to find the exact location in every case – but you will be 'very warm'. The listings under each area are arranged to make as walkable a route as possible.

Cemeteries are listed separately at the end of this guide.

CENTRAL LONDON

Soho/Piccadilly/St James's/Mayfair
Oxford Street (John Lewis), W1 – Barbara Hepworth
Dean Street, W1 – Eleanor Marx
Wardour Street (St Anne's Church), W1 – Dorothy L. Sayers
Haymarket (Theatre Royal), SW1 – Lady Bancroft; Frances Abington
Haymarket (Her Majesty's Theatre), SW1 – Arabella Goddard
Waterloo Place, SW1 – Florence Nightingale; Lady Kennet
Carlton House Terrace, SW1 – Catherine Gladstone; Mary Somerville
The Mall (Marlborough House), SW1 – Sarah, Duchess of Marlborough
Pall Mall (Schomberg House), SW1 – Ann Curtis
St James's Square, SW1 – Nancy, Lady Astor
St James's Place, SW1 – Hester Chapone
Jermyn Street (Cavendish Hotel, rebuilt), SW1 – Rosa Lewis
Piccadilly (St James's Church), SW1 – Mary Delany; Mary Beale
Piccadilly (Royal Academy of Art), W1 – Angelica Kauffmann; Margaret
    Carpenter; Lady Elizabeth Butler
Conduit Street, W1 – Harriet Martineau
St George Street (St George's Church), W1 – Elinor Glyn; Amy Johnson
South Audley Street (Grosvenor Chapel), W1 – Lady Mary Wortley
    Montagu; Elizabeth Carter
South Street, W1 – Catherine Walters; Florence Nightingale
Bolton Street, W1 – Fanny Burney

Marylebone
Seymour Place, W1 – Emma Cons
Gloucester Place, W1 – Mary Anne Clarke
Montagu Square, W1 – Lady Hester Stanhope
Cavendish Square, W1 – Lady Charlotte Guest
Wimpole Street W1 and Marylebone Road (St Marylebone Church),
    NW1 – Elizabeth Barrett Browning
Harley Street, W1 – Dorothea Beale; Gertrude Bell; Jane Digby
Portland Place, W1 – Frances Hodgson Burnett; Elizabeth Scott
Langham Place (All Souls' Church), W1 – Nancy, Lady Astor

Also in Central London
Paddington Green (St Mary's Church), W2 – Sarah Siddons

Bloomsbury
Fitzroy Square, W1 – Virginia Woolf; Vanessa Bell
Whitfield Street, W1 – Marie Stopes
Bedford Square, WC1 – Lady Ottoline Morrell
Gower Street, WC1 – Millicent Garrett Fawcett
Gower Street (Slade School of Art), WC1 – Dora Carrington; Gwen John
Gower Street (University College), WC1 – Dame Kathleen Lonsdale
Great Russell Street (British Museum), WC1 – Anne Seymour Damer
Torrington Square, WC1 – Christina Rossetti
Gordon Square, WC1 – Lady Jane Strachey; Vanessa Bell
Tavistock Square, WC1 – Louisa Aldrich-Blake
Endsleigh Street, WC1 – Dorothy Richardson
Handel Street (St George's Gardens) WC1 – Nancy Dawson

Leicester Square/Covent Garden
Leicester Square, WC2 – Kate Hamilton
St Martin's Place, WC2 – Edith Cavell
Strand (Charing Cross Station), WC2 – Queen Eleanor
Henrietta Street, WC2 – Jane Austen
St Paul's Church (Covent Garden), WC2 – Betty Careless; Lilian Baylis;
   Vivien Leigh; Sophie Fedorovitch; Ellen Terry; Edith Evans
Bow Street/Floral Street (Royal Opera House), WC2 – Martha Reay;
   Elizabeth Billington; Kathleen Ferrier
Bow Street, WC2 – Mary Ann Talbot
Drury Lane, WC2 – Nell Gwyn
Lincoln's Inn Fields, WC2 – Margaret MacDonald
Strand (St Clement Dane's Church), WC2 – Mrs Thrale
Strand (near St Mary-le-Strand), WC2 – Lottie Collins

Whitehall/Westminster
Whitehall – Lady Caroline Lamb
Whitehall (and Whitehall Theatre), SW1 – Phyllis Dixey
Westminster Bridge, SW1 – Boudicca (or Boadicea)
House of Commons (Houses of Parliament), SW1 – Nancy Astor, Ellen
   Wilkinson
Millbank (Victoria Tower Gardens), SW1 – Emmeline and Christabel
   Pankhurst
Westminster Abbey, SW1 – Angela Burdett-Coutts; Lady Margaret
   Beaufort; the Brontë sisters; Jane Austen; George Eliot; Dorothy
   Osborne; Elizabeth I; Mary Tudor; Queen Eleanor; Aphra Behn; Anne
   Bracegirdle; Anne Oldfield; Long Meg of Westminster; Frances,
   Duchess of Richmond and Lennox
Dean's Yard, Westminster, SW1 – Alice Hargreaves
Queen Anne's Gate, SW1 – Queen Anne

WEST LONDON

Pimlico/Chelsea
Vincent Square, SW1 – Pocohontas
Claverton Street, SW1 – Adelaide Bartlett
Swan Walk and Chelsea Physic Gardens, SW3 – Elizabeth Blackwell
Cheyne Walk, SW3 – George Eliot; Elizabeth Gaskell; Queen Katherine
   Parr
Cheyne Row, SW3 – Jane Carlyle; Margaret Damer Dawson
Chelsea Embankment (Chelsea Old Church and Crosby Hall) SW3 –
   Mary Astell; Elizabeth Blackwell; Margaret Roper
Royal Hospital Road (Royal Hospital, Chelsea), SW3 – Christian Davis
Sloane Court, SW3 – Katherine Furse
King's Road, SW3 – Princess Astafieva; Ellen Terry

Belgravia/Kensington
Draycott Terrace (St Mary's Church) SW3 – Madame Tussaud
Chester Square, SW1 – Mary Shelley
Cadogan Place, SW1 – Dorothy Jordan
Pont Street, SW1 – Lillie Langtry
Hans Place, SW1 – Jane Austen
Onslow Square, SW7 and Young Street, W8 – Anne Ritchie
Kensington Square, W8 – Mrs Patrick Campbell
Palace Gate, W8 – Effie Millais; Violet Van der Elst
The Broad Walk (Kensington Gardens) W8 – Queen Victoria
Kensington Gore (Royal Albert Hall), SW7 – Clara Butt; Marguerite
   Gardiner; Ethel Smyth
Hyde Park, SW7/W2 – Celia Fiennes; Adeline Horsey de Horsey;
   Catherine Walters; Harriet Shelley

Bayswater
Palace Court, W2 – Alice Meynell
Porchester Terrace, W2 – Jane Loudon

Also in West London
Longridge Road, SW5 – Marie Corelli
Chiswick Mall, W4 – Barbara Villiers

NORTH LONDON

Euston
Euston Road (Elizabeth Garrett Anderson Hospital), NW1 – Elizabeth
  Garrett Anderson; Louisa Aldrich-Blake
Pancras Road (St Pancras Gardens), NW1 – Jenny Diver; Mary Flaxman;
  Mary Wollstonecraft

Hampstead
South Hill Park (Magdala Pub), NW3 – Ruth Ellis
Keats Grove, NW3 – Fanny Brawne
East Heath Road, NW3 – Katherine Mansfield
Church Row, NW3 – Anna Barbauld
Church Row (St John's Church), NW3 and Windmill Hill (Bolton
  House), NW3 – Joanna Baillie
Frognal, NW3 – Kathleen Ferrier; Kate Greenaway

St John's Wood
Primrose Hill Road, NW3 – Helen Waddell
Netherhall Gardens, NW3 – Beatrice Webb
Langford Place, NW8 – Dame Laura Knight
Cunningham Place, NW8 – Emily Davies
St John's Wood Church Gardens, NW8 – Joanna Southcott

Highgate
Southwood Lane, N6 – Mary Kingsley
Highgate Cemetery, Swains Lane, N6 – SEE 'CEMETERIES'

Golders Green
Golders Green Crematorium, NW11 – Elinor Glyn; Philippa Fawcett;
  Nellie Wallace
Golders Green Cemetery (West London Synagogue), NW11 – Julia
  Goodman

Also in North London
Parkhurst Road (Holloway Prison), N7 – Emily Davison; Ruth Ellis;
  Edith Thompson
Stoke Newington (Abney Park Cemetery), N16 – Anna Barbauld;
  Catherine Booth; Rebecca Jarrett

**EAST LONDON
(The City of London)**

Crown Office Row, EC4 – Mary Lamb
Temple Lane (and Temple Church) EC4 – Sarah Malcolm, Margaret
  Godolphin
Fleet Street, EC4 – Lady Kennet; Elizabeth I; Mary Frith
Ludgate Hill (site of old Ludgate/Fleet prison), EC4 – Kat Astley; Agnes
  Forster
St Paul's Cathedral, EC4 – Queen Anne; Florence Nightingale (crypt)
Amen Corner, EC4 – Mary Hughes
Old Bailey (Central Criminal Court), EC4 – Ruth Ellis; Elizabeth Fry;
  Adelaide Bartlett; Ethel le Neve; Edith Thompson
Newgate Street (Christ Church) EC1 – Elizabeth Barton; Lady Venetia
  Digby
Aldersgate Street (Postman's Park), EC1 – Mary Rogers
West Smithfield, EC1 – Anne Askew; Dr Elizabeth Blackwell

Bunhill Fields, EC1 – Catherine Blake; Dame Mary Page
Milk Street, EC2 – Isabella Beeton
Poultry (St Mildred's Court), EC2 – Elizabeth Fry
Cornhill, EC3 – The Brontës
Hart Street (St Olave's Church), EC3 – Elizabeth Pepys; Elizabeth Fry;
    Josephine Butler; Florence Nightingale; Edith Cavell: Stained-glass
    window
The Tower of London, EC3 – Anne Boleyn; Lady Jane Grey; Lucy
    Hutchinson

Also in East London
Graham Road, Hoxton, E8 – Marie Lloyd
Hackney Road (Queen Elizabeth Hospital) E2 – Sarah Heckford

SOUTH LONDON
Waterloo Road (Old Vic Theatre), SE1 – Emma Cons; Lilian Baylis
Lambeth Palace Road (St Thomas's Hospital), SE1 – Florence Nightingale
Lambeth Palace Road (Lambeth Palace), SE1 – Maria Edgeworth; Annie
    Kenney
Lambeth Road (St Mary-at-Lambeth Church), SE1 – Eleanor Coade and
    her daughter Eleanor
Lambeth Road (Imperial War Museum), SE1 – Edith Cavell; Flora Sandes
Southwark Bridge Road (Southwark Cathedral), SE1 – Mary, the
    Ferryman's Daughter

Also in South London
Colby Road, SE19 – Annie Besant
Norwood High Street (South Metropolitan Cemetery), SE27 – Isabella
    Beeton
Greenwich (St Alphage Church), SE10 – Lavinia Fenton
Burnley Road, Brixton, SW9 – Violette Szabo
Stockwell Park Road, SW9 – Lilian Baylis
Mortlake Road (Mortlake Cemetery), SW14 – Isabel Burton
Merton Road, Merton (St Mary the Virgin Church), SW19 – Emma
    Hamilton

**JUST OUTSIDE
LONDON**
Hampton Court Palace, Hampton Court, Kingston-upon-Thames – Mary
    Fitton; Mary, Countess of Pembroke; Sibel Penne
High Street, Teddington, Middlesex – Peg Woffington
St Mary's Church, Twickenham, Middlesex – Kitty Clive
Ham House, Richmond, Surrey – Elizabeth Dysart
Paradise Road, Richmond, Surrey – Virginia Woolf
St Mary's Church, Richmond, Surrey – Mary Braddon; Mary Ann Yates
Kew Gardens, Richmond, Surrey – Marianne North
Theydon Bois, near Epping – Frances Buss

CEMETERIES

It is exceptionally difficult to track down individual graves in the larger London cemeteries. However, this should not deter anyone from exploring these fascinating and almost forgotten areas.

The major cemeteries in London are Brompton, Kensal Green and Highgate.

Brompton Cemetery, West Brompton, SW6 – Lady Bancroft; Fanny Brawne; Blanche Macchetta; Emmeline Pankhurst

Kensal Green Cemetery (including St Mary's Roman Catholic Cemetery), Harrow Road, NW10 – Dr James Barry; Maria, Lady Calcott; Anna Jameson; Fanny Kemble; Jane Loudon; Emma Soyer; Madame Vestris; Christine Granville; Alice Meynell

Highgate Cemetery, Swains Lane, N6
Highgate Cemetery is divided by Swains Lane into two sections – East and West. The East section is normally open during daytime hours. The West section is normally closed, but has an occasional 'open day'. For details contact: The Hon Secretary, Friends of Highgate Cemetery, 5 View Road, Highgate, N6.

East Section: – Catherine Booth Clibborn; George Eliot; Eleanor Marx

West Section: – Anne Bartholomew; Catherine Dickens; Radclyffe Hall; Elizabeth Lilly; Christina Rossetti; Elizabeth Siddal; Ellen Wood